The Papers of John Marsh Smith, 1849-1857

Transcribed and Annotated
by
The Historical Activities Committee
of
The National Society of The Colonial Dames of America
in the State of Oregon

Portland, Oregon

The Historical Activities Committee:

Nancy Horton Bragdon
Ann Brewster Clarke
Elizabeth Kelley Crookham
Frances Novy Diack
Elizabeth Griffin Hampson
Ma'Carry Webster Hull
Anne Maloon Kingery
Katherine Reese Pamplin
Elizabeth Minott Wessinger
Helen Malarkey Thompson, *chairman*

The National Society of The Colonial Dames of America
in the State of Oregon
c/o Oregon Historical Society
1230 S.W. Park
Portland, OR 97205-2483

John Marsh Smith

Many years ago I was given this oil portrait of John Marsh Smith, my great-grandfather. He is shown therein as clothed in red flannels and a suit of buckskin and holding a rifle. For a family of Quaker background, this was most unusual. Even stranger was the fact that there were many holes in the canvas, made by arrowheads.

Later, I had the painting restored and the canvas mended, and also learned the explanation for its battlescars. It seems that a group of John Marsh Smith's grandsons were playing "Cowboys and Indians," and got so excited and let their imaginations so run away with them that they shot Great-Grandfather's portrait in a most un-Quakerish way.

I suppose many young Quaker men in 1848 dreamed of finding gold in the hills of the West instead of tending store in Baltimore or Philadelphia, but very few tried it. John Marsh Smith did. Did this spirit of adventure find a distant echo in his grandsons' bow-and-arrow assault on his portrait?

John L. Clark

PREFACE

IN 1933, JANIE SMITH Taliaferro gave to The National Society of The Colonial Dames of America in the State of Oregon a collection of letters. Most of them were written by her father, John Marsh Smith, to her mother and other family members and friends in Baltimore, and recounted his experiences in the California gold fields and in Oregon between 1849 and 1851. Included were letters sent to him. These caught him up with family news, conveyed business requests, and later, when he had left the territory, kept him in touch with life out west as Oregon moved toward statehood.

For more than 50 years the collection has been in the custody of the Oregon Historical Society. In 1980 it was used for a course in historical materials taught by Dr. Allan Kittell at Lewis and Clark College. In 1984 the Historical Activities Chairman of the Colonial Dames in Oregon was asked to form a committee to study the letters with the possibility of publishing them. As research progressed, enthusiasm mounted and the book has indeed evolved.

We are indebted to Dr. Kittell; to Peter Cook, assistant director of writing and research; and to the members of the Lewis and Clark class for much of the information that supplements the letters in this book. Special thanks must go to committee member Ma'Carry Hull, who has followed each reference to its source, and, through long hours of individual research, has interpreted for our under-standing the period during which the letters were written.

To convey the flavor of the correspondence, we have endeavored to maintain the original spelling, punctuation and usage as much as possible, making alterations only in the interest of clarity. With the exception of some minor changes, the letters are here presented as written.

Some of the letters in the collection appear to be handwritten copies made by a family member—perhaps Harriet Tyson—to share with the rest of the family; some are typewritten copies, made at Mrs. Taliaferro's request, before she gave the collection to the Colonial Dames in Oregon. Omitted from this publication are mis-cellaneous invoices, bills of lading and notes of personal purchases by John Marsh Smith.

We are deeply grateful to Judge John L. Clark of Baltimore, great-grandson of John Marsh Smith, for his interest, support and cooper-ation in supplying us with pertinent details and family photographs.

We thank members of the staff of the Oregon Historical Society for their unfailing help: Thomas Vaughan, director; Bruce Hamil-ton, director of the society's press; and Edith Farrar, Margaret Haines, Priscilla Knuth, George Manning, and Charles Wellman.

We also thank the staff of the San Diego Historical Society; The Bancroft Library of the University of California at Berkeley; the Yuba County Library in Marysville, California; and the Multnomah County Library in Portland, Oregon.

Our committee member Elizabeth Crookham drew the small pic-tures that embellish the text; for these she receives our warmest thanks.

Financial assistance from The National Society of The Colonial Dames of America and from the S. S. Johnson Foundation has helped make possible the publication of these letters.

Finally, we wish to thank our professionals: Susan Applegate, Philippa Brunsman, John Tomlinson, and Melissa Wells. They have guided, supported, and sustained us.

The Historical Activities Committee of
The National Society of The Colonial Dames of America
in the State of Oregon

CONTENTS

Introduction   **1**
Chapter One: 1849   **5**
Chapter Two: 1850   **45**
Chapter Three: 1851   **123**
Chapter Four: 1852   **155**
Chapter Five: 1853-1857   **161**
Sources   **167**
Family Tree   **170**
Appendix: Excerpts from *Eldorado* by Bayard Taylor   **173**
Index   **187**

MAPS

J. Marsh Smith's Travels: 1849-1851   **3**
The Isthmus of Panama: 1849-1851   **16**
J. Marsh Smith's California: 1849-1851   **57**
J. Marsh Smith's Oregon Territory in 1850   **115**

ILLUSTRATIONS

Incident on the Chagres River   **20**
Sacramento During the Great Inundation   **50**
San Francisco Post Office   **53**

Dear Lizzie

INTRODUCTION

On June 27 1849, John Marsh Smith, a 30-year-old Quaker from Baltimore, left home with his younger brother-in-law Frederick Tyson, to look for gold in California. The pair were representative of a large segment of 49ers who came from comfortably settled middle-class backgrounds, as opposed to the footloose adventurers generally considered typical of the period.

JMS left behind his wife, Elizabeth Brooke Tyson Smith, and two small sons, to whom he was deeply devoted. In his letters to "Dear Lizzie" and to other family members and friends during the next two years, he describes his journey to the gold fields, which he did not reach until February 1850. The trip from New York, down the East Coast by steamer to Chagres, across the Isthmus of Panama, and up the West Coast to San Francisco, took two months. In San Francisco, JMS became associated with Joseph Hobson of Cross, Hobson & Company, merchants, through his acquaintance with Hobson's brother William, a family friend. During this association, he travelled to Monterey and to Sacramento, where, for a short time, he ran a hotel, partially financed by William Hobson. The hotel failed, perhaps as much because JMS did not condone gambling, which seems to have been a requisite for success, as because the owners decided to sell.

1

In January 1850, Sacramento was inundated by a disastrous flood. Meanwhile, Fred Tyson had gone to Mormon Island, near Sutter's Mill, one of the most populous gold-mining camps, where he was joined by JMS. Both men had had bouts of illness, and Fred was still in poor health when JMS, leaving him to recover, joined a group of "perfect gentlemen" to prospect in the hills near Georgetown. It was during this period that he began his diary, which is an intrinsic part of this record.

By mid-April, Fred was sufficiently restored to join the group, but almost immediately suffered so severe a relapse that JMS was obliged to expend what meager profits he had realized from his labors on securing Fred's recovery and sending him home.

After Fred's departure in June, JMS went briefly into business with James Suydam of New York. However, business was "dull," and Sacramento's climate proved to be unhealthy. His many friends urged JMS to try his luck in Oregon, and by late September he was on his way north. His journey was plagued by dangers that are characteristically understated in his subsequent letter to Lizzie.

During his months in Oregon, he made the acquaintance of Dr. John McLoughlin, the former Hudson's Bay Company factor at Fort Vancouver, and of Hugh Burns, an Irishman from Missouri, whose donation land claim lay along the Willamette River across from Oregon City. His letters home during the period contain a succinct analysis of trade in the Oregon Territory. In February 1851, he wrote Lizzie from Astoria to say that he would return home in the fall if he did not succeed in business or if he failed to be appointed marshal of the Oregon Territory, a position for which he had entertained ambition. But the death of his brother-in-law James Atkinson decided him. He was needed at home, and thence he repaired.

These letters to "Dear Lizzie" portray the writer as a man of keen sensibilities. His Quaker upbringing is evident in his moral rectitude, his concern for others, and his loving tenderness toward Lizzie and the "dear little boys." Throughout the letters there is a delightful thread of humor. One wishes that Lizzie's letters in response might be included in this book, but, alas, they have disappeared.

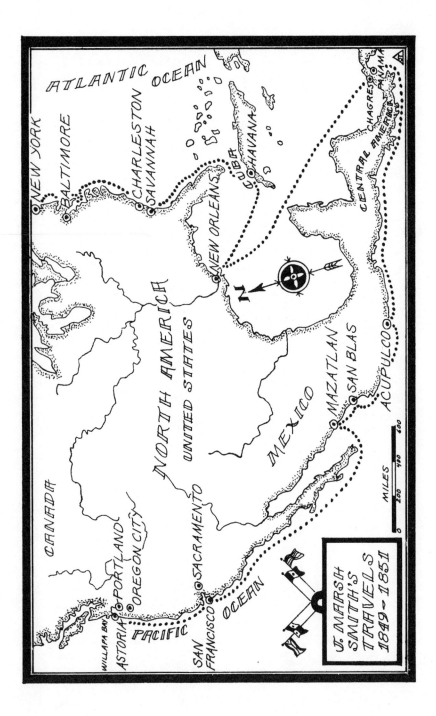

ATLANTIC OCEAN

NEW YORK
BALTIMORE
CHARLESTON
SAVANNAH
NEW ORLEANS
CUBA
HAVANNA
CHAGRES
PANAMA
CENTRAL AMERICA

NORTH AMERICA
UNITED STATES

MEXICO

MAZATLAN
SAN BLAS
ACUPULCO

CANADA

PORTLAND
OREGON CITY
WILLAPA BAY
ASTORIA
SACRAMENTO
SAN FRANCISCO
PACIFIC OCEAN

MILES
0 200 400 600

J. MARSH
SMITH'S
TRAVELS
1849~1851

3

CHAPTER ONE
1849

· · · · ·

Washington, June 22 1849

To Col. James Corwin
San Francisco, California
DEAR COL.

This will introduce you to *my* friend & *my wife's* Cousin Js M. Smith of Balt[imore]. He comes to you & your far off Provence, to look into the great El Dorado of the 19th Century.

He has been bred a Merchant, his Father & Mother are of the Quaker School. Smith is honest in the old fashioned sense of that much abused word.

I pray you give him such counsel as to his ability in California & his needs & as you alone can give. You will thus confer a favor on a deserving man & oblige your *old* but sincere friend.

Thos Corwin

· · · · ·

Washington D.C., June 1849

To Gen'l Jno Wilson
Superintendent of Indian Affairs
San Francisco, California
DEAR GEN'L.

This letter will be handed to you by my friend, John M. Smith of Baltimore, Md.

He visits your Colony on business. He can, I doubt not, be greatly benefitted by your kindly attentions & especially by suggestions your ample knowledge of the country may enable you to *make* to him as the object of his enterprise.

I feel a [illegible] interest in his success. He is a very worthy & perfectly trustworthy man. I know him well. Besides he is the cousin of my wife & a certain respect for the latter ables me to like her friends.

I have to ask as a favor to him & a personal one to myself, that you will give him the benefit of your regards while he remains in the territory.

TRULY YOUR FRIEND,
Wm. Corwin

· · · · ·

Baltimore, June 25 1849

To Capt. Gustav Van Tempsky
San Francisco
MY DEAR SIR

This letter will be handed you by Mr. J. Marsh Smith, who goes out, as you have done, to push his fortune in El Dorado, and whose acquaintance I have had the pleasure of making through the kindness of Mr. Pearce. I hope you will have an opportunity of cultivating Mr. Smith's acquaintance, and that you will derive pleasure from it, as I expect.

I remain, my dear sir,
YOURS SINCERELY
Jas. Stanislaw Bell

· · · · ·

New York, June 27 1849

To Elizabeth Brooke Smith
DEAR LIZZIE

Without much to communicate but simply to advise thee of our safe arrival in this great Babel, without adventure of any character save the torturous solicitations of the professional Hackmen, who seem to think if they succeed in placing their card in your hand they then have a claim upon you that nought but an acceptance of the services will compromise, and then assume upon themselves the responsibility of throwing your baggage about as though trunks were invulnerable, valuables were made no more to break, and owners had no feelings. I am in hopes I may have as pressing invitations crossing the Isthmus for the same jobs.

I felt so fatigued on my arrival at Philadelphia that I kept myself quiet during my stay there and intend as much as possible to do so here. Fred seems remarkably well.[1] All I want is two or three days rest, then, "Richard will be himself again." I understood from Fred that all our friends in Philadelphia were out of town. George Martin, young Hallowell, and some of Fred's friends came down to the boat to see us off.[2]

I was much gratified on arriving at the water station to find Harry there with a letter from Anne reporting all well and dear little Gill first rate, amusing Hannah by blowing Soap Bubbles.[3] I expect to write again before we sail.

With love to all. Tell mother that in the hurry and confusion Lewis Cass lost his reasoning facultys and I fear I have lost the direction to the cousin Ivesy.[4] I want to see them and will look for there residence in directory.

THINE AFFECTIONATELY
J.M. Smith

· · · · ·

New York Steamer *Falcon*,[5] June 28 1849

To Elizabeth Brooke Smith
DEAR LIZZIE

I recd thy favour this morning, am delighted to find thee bears my departure so well. I have been a little under the weather for the last two days but I am now right well. Fatigue and a bile in the old locality were the causes of my indisposition.[6] I wrote Mother this morning. Fred has gone out to make some purchases. Amongst others I remind him of the life preservers. My love to all. Adieu. The news from California's most flattering.

THY AFFECTIONATE HUSBAND
J. Marsh Smith

· · · · ·

Off Sandy Hook 20 miles, June 28, 1849

To Elizabeth Brooke Smith
DEAR LIZZIE

Things are quivering so on board of Steamer it is hard to write with a steady hand. We are just about putting pilot off. Prospect of fine weather. I feel first rate. The sight of the sea is as a charm. I am right well bar[r]ing the bile, for which I am prepaired, having a lot of flax seed meal with me. Adieu. If we should stop at Charleston will try and mail thee another.

love to all
THY AFFECTIONATE HUSBAND
J. M. Smith

· · · · ·

To Elizabeth Brooke Smith

DEAR LIZZIE

I commence by excusing myself for the careless manner in which I expect to pen this epistle. The ship is pitching, rendering it difficult to write. Probably I may succeed better than I anticipate in shaping my letters. The day is delightfull, the sea air most bracing. I feel as though I had gained a pound or two since I left New York.

The accounts we gather on board from persons who have been to California are of the most encouraging kind. I feel more ardent in the cause since I left home than before I started. I am perfectly easy about you all and have the consolation of finding most of our passengers are men who have left families behind, similar to myself, but none with better or more kind Friends. One of the lady passengers we have is on her return from N York to N Orleans, having accompanied her Husband as far as the former, from whence he sailed for a three years cruise, he being an officer in the Navy. She returns in chge of the Captain.

There is something remarkable in the increase of the mail to California. The first mail this ship carried out was taken over the Isthmus under a man's arm, the second some fifteen hundred letters, the third five thousand, fourth Ten thousand, and this the fifth with only the mail from N York is all ready Fifteen Thousand. We have yet to get mails from Charleston, Savannah, Havannah, N. Orleans, and Chagres.[7]

I cannot help thinking and feeling for you how you are suffering in Friends' meeting at this time with the heat, while I am enjoying the delightfull temperature and air of the Ocean. There is no scarcity of Smiths on this ship. Five I know of and one of the passengers that I have formed as favourable an opinion of as I ever did of a Stranger is a John Smith, a brother of an army officer who has been ordered out, a Major Smith. I am quite encouraged. A Captain Skenk of the Navy told me that Smith was a good name in California, that all he knew there had made a good deal of money, and he thought the luck would continue if all the Smiths that went there should be such as we have on board of this ship at this time. We have a genteel representation. Major Smith is a perfect Gentleman and his brother John a young man of very much William Mastier's appearance and character. We have struck up quite an intimacy. He expects to go digging, and the Major, going out on different duty, goes unprepared for any such operation, but says if he finds treasure he shall depend on me for one of my picks as I have three.

Please write immediately on recpt of this and direct to New Orleans. I will call and enquire at the Saint Charles Hotel where thee had better direct "J.Marsh Smith passenger on *Falcon* to be called for at St. Charles Hotel."[8] We will stop in Orleans a day or so to coal. Thee need not give Thyself any uneasiness about my health there. I will take good care of myself as regards exposure and diet. We have had no sickness on board excepting sea sickness since I came on board. We have as temperate and moral a set of passengers fore and aft as was ever on a sea steamers deck. We number about seventy.

With love to all and a kiss for the little boys I close for the present. I expect to write from Orleans where we will be about Monday or Tuesday of next week (not this week).

THY AFFECTIONATE
J. Marsh Smith

To Catherine Marsh Smith[9]

dear Mother if thee was on board of this ship thee would enjoy it exceedingly. I will write thee soon. It consumes all the genius I am possessed of at present to manufacture a letter for Lizzie.

THY SON
JMS

· · · · ·

To Elizabeth Brooke Smith

DEAR LIZZIE

At half past five this afternoon we passed under the celebrated Moro Castle, which is without doubt one of the most stupendous works of the kind it has ever been my lot to gaze upon. It is built on the sea side upon solid rock with a front of, some say at a guess, three hundred feet, and on the side fronting the town an extent of half a mile, with as I understand subterraneous passages to the extent of Seven Miles.

We are denied the pleasure of exploring what I should judge to be a magnificent city, owing to the circumstance of cholera in New York, the city we cleared from. It is amusing to see with what horror they approach us, fear depicted not only in their countenances but in their manners. The doctor did not board us—the nearest anyone has been to us is boat hook length. They have a pair of tongs at the end of a long pole in which I saw placed the customs house papers. Before they were opened they were sprinkled with what I understood was vinegar, and to clap the climax a couple of instruments were passed on board in these remarkable tongs, for puncturing the letters intended for Havanna. They are to be rubbed before delivered in chloride of Lime. They stick them to let the cholera air out. Is it not remarkable?

FRIDAY NIGHT, JULY 6. This day at one o'clock we bid adieu to Havanna. From the poor opportunity I had of judging, I conceive it to be a magnificent city with a population, as I understand, of, near one hundred and eighty thousand and probably one of the most compact but beautiful Harbours in the world. It looks more to me like a wash basin with the bottom covered with water than anything else I can compare it to, its sides dotted with the beautiful residences of its wealthy citizens, all around is covered with the richest verdure. There is not one barren or unproductive spot for the eye to rest upon. All is magnificantly rich. I understand from some Spanish passengers we are carrying to Orleans that they would like to be governed by some power more liberal than Old Spain.

It is now 10 oclock, night and I feel like retiring. We are making most beautiful progress at the time with a glorious breeze off the quarter—Steam on and all sail set going at the rate of 12 knots an hour. Trusting you are all well and happy, I bid adieu for the night to retire with the anticipation of a delightful nights repose.

SATURDAY NIGHT, 10 OCLOCK. Before I retire I will write a few words. As I anticipated last night, I slept delightfully. We have had the weather exceedingly pleasant since we left the sultry harbor of Havanna. I really think from the way that I feel that I must have gained several pounds since I left home, and as for Fred he is so fat that every thing appears tight for him, and if he continues to grow in the same ratio for a week or two, he will soon be too big for his blanket. Goodnight.

SUNDAY NIGHT, 1/2 PAST 9 OCLOCK. Dear Lizzie, Fred and myself are both enjoying good health. We are feeling our way up the "giraffe of waters" [Mississippi River]. I find amongst our passengers the young man who wrote the travels of a tour through Germany on foot, Bayard Taylor.[10] He goes out on an expedition of a similar kind to California. He is, I believe, a correspondent for the [New York] *Tribune*, and I think a weekly *Tribune* may give you a better account of our adventures than I can. By my side is a John Smith penning a few lines to his mother. He is a perfect Gentleman and an honour to the name.

Goodnight Lizzie, with prayers that you may all be protected. Kiss the little boys but do not talk of my absence to them.

MONDAY NIGHT. Dear Lizzie, I am very comfortably moored on shore. We had quite a delightful sail up the Mississippi and as there was some sickness on board the steamer, and leaving New Orleans was perfectly clear of cholera and yellow fever, it was considered advisable by us nearly all fore and aft to spend a few days on shore.

There is about fifty of us comfortably quartered at the great St. Charles. Do not feel any uneasiness about us. I have met several of my old acquaintances here and they assure me New Orleans was never known to be more healthy. We were so unfortunate as to loose two men on our passage out: one a fireman, the other a cook. The place where they worked, the thermometer stood at one hundred and thirty degrees, [and they were] drinking ice water profusely. Do not feel any uneasiness about me. I do consider myself cautious. Some few of the passengers have been attacked with cholera symptoms, but it has yielded readily to simple remedies.

Things happen strange. Thee recollects a couple of Gentlemen by the name of Smith from near Chester? They were with us a day or so at Osceola.[11] Well, a Major Hays of the Army who tells me he will leave in the morning has given me a letter of introduction to the largest one.[12] Thee recollects he was quite a robust, fine looking young fellow. [He] says I will find him a perfect Gentleman and desirable acquaintance. He also gives me a letter to the Commisary at Saint Francis[co] which says he will be of service to me. I have been treated kindly by everybody—no one has asked me to lend them money, and need not. I feel as though my motto was "go ahead." Good night.

TUESDAY MORNING, JULY 10. I am happy to report a delightful night's rest. A refreshing bath and first rate breakfast causes an individual to feel a little saucy, am proud to say that I have not been bitten by a single mosquito, while some of my companions have been compelled to use ammonia most lavishly. I made up my mind to sleep on board of ship to night but Captain Codman, an old traveller, advises by all means not to give up the Comfortable quarters I am occupying as the change on shore, with a moderate use of its comforts, will be worth more to us all than it is probable it will cost.

I have just been introduced to a gentleman that arrived in a steamer last night from Chagres. He says there was not a single person waiting at Panama, that there were four steamers expected, that the steamer *Oris* was running up to Cruces, that there were canoes and mules enough to carry 500 passengers over.[13] There was no sickness on the Isthmus excepting Ague at Chagres, where we would not be detained.[14] The Gentleman I spoke of brought a lady over the Isthmus with him. She is a sister of William Hobson's wife.[15] William and his wife are in San Francisco. He gives me great encouragement.

Love to all. I will write Mother before I leave. Remember me to my kind friends, and [I] hardly know how to express my thanks to Thos. M., Uncle Thomas, J. Curlitt, Talbott, Robert and James, Mother, Father and all.[16] I hope I will prove myself worthy of their kindness. Be happy. Kiss the little boys. Remember me to them all at home, Jericho, and regards for all that may ask after me.[17] Fred is well and wrote yesterday.

Excuse many defects. I am aware of many and think it will be advisable to read this letter, [rather] than to have it read. I find a good many like myself that say they cannot write.

THY AFFECTIONATE
John Marsh Smith

New Orleans, July 10 1849

I expect I should receive a letter from home before we leave N. Orleans, as The Captain has informed me we'll not sail before Friday. The passengers are all growling at the manner we have been treated by the agents of the steamer. I tell them I shall not complain until I find how the thing ends. Our detention may be for the best.

JMS

· · · · ·

New Orleans, July 13 1849

To Elizabeth Brooke Smith
DEAR LIZZIE

I yesterday handed Jonathan Janny a letter for Mother with one or two little trifles which will probably be received before thee gets this, as I intend forwarding this by mail, and mails are not as regular in this country as they ought to be.

I went down to the ship yesterday and the passengers who had remained on board presented such a terrific appearance, from innumerable wounds rec'd from some Individuals from amongst the Myriads of blood sucking Musquitois. Having spent a comfortable and pleasant time here, I thought it would be wrong to mar its pleasures, so I verry quickly made up my mind to return and spend the night in comfortable quarters. I have not been disappointed. After a delightfull night's rest, I report at 6 oclock, myself up and penning to thee. Our stay in New Orleans, I think, has been of great service to me.

This N Orleans is a remarkable place. Dissipation seems to occupy the leisure moments of the great Mass here. The Magnificances and Immence size of its drinking saloons and the momentum of business in that line is astounding. I cant think that any man can like N Orleans that does not like dissipation. They have churches here, but I fear Christianity is kept behind the curtain. As Jimmy Kernan says, "I [Aye], it is looked upon as a mere superstition."

With love to all. Good by, be happy.

THINE

J Marsh Smith

Fred is well. I have not rec'd any letter since I have been here.

• • • • •

Panama, July 28 1849

To Elizabeth Brooke Smith
Bayles and Tyson
Baltimore, Maryland, U States
[Forwarded to] Care of Nathan Tyson
Jerusalem Mills
Harford Co., Md.
DEAR LIZZIE

All here is confusion, I write in great haste simply stating that Fred and myself have got along this far as well as any of the *Falcon* passengers. The *Crescent City* passengers have nearly all left or are comfortably provided for.[18] We pay them 30¢ to pay for our room and get our meals for 20¢ each. As regards the health of the place, it is good.

It is as much as one person can do here to look out for themselves. I purchased a steerage ticket here this morning for 300 dollars and leave in the morning for San Francisco. Fred probably will leave in the steamer if he can succeed in purchasing a ticket. A gentleman from Maryland, an acquaintance of mine, promises to forward our Bagg[age] none of which has arrived.

Send word to Henry Warfield if he should conclude to cross the Isthmus by no means to bring more baggage than he can carry on his arm.[19] Tell him I have been so engaged I have not had time to write him.

ATLANTIC OCEAN

CHAGRES

AREA OF
LARGE MAP

PANAMA
1:12 000 000

N

RIO CHAGRES

RIO CHAGRES

CRUCES

GORGONA

THE
ISTHMUS
OF PANAMA
1849-1851

RIO PANAMA

PANAMA

MILES
0   5   10

PACIFIC OCEAN

I leave Fred, if he is compelled to stop here, in charge of Doct McMullen of the Army, an acquaintance of mine I made in N Orleans, said to be one of the most distinguished Doctors in the Army, [a] "perfect gentleman," for should Fred get sick which I do not anticipate he will receive every care. I make arrangement for Fred to room with him.

Give my love and Kiss the little boys. May God Bless you all. I am bound to California and expect to meet with difficulty but would not turn back for less than 25 thousand till I give California a trial. I am as happy as one can be who has left all he loves behind. Give love to all at home, at Jericho, every where. Fred will finish this. I have a letter written already to enclude but it is with my baggage which I trust may come to hand.

THINE
J M Smith

[The following is on the same sheet.]

Panama, July 28 1849

To Elizabeth Brooke Smith
MY DEAR SISTER

John has written the above in great haste having just procured a ticket on board the *Panama* for California, which vessel will sail early tomorrow morning.[20] Our baggage has not yet come on. I cannot succeed in getting a ticket for the *Panama*. They have been asking one hundred to one hundred and fifty percent advance on the original fee of the ticket and are none to be had at present for any price. John has enough clothes with him to make himself comfortable and besides has many staunch friends who have been passengers from N York with us who will not let him want for anything.

We would not have separated but for the Impossibility of going on together as all our baggage is behind, and if tickets were even to be had, it would be best for one to stay behind and take care of it. I anticipate no difficulty in getting on as the *Oregon* Steamer is here and will sail in two or three weeks. There are also two sailing vessels left that will take off a great number of passengers, and the steamer *Unicorn* is daily expected.

We had rather a rough time in crossing the Isthmus. If I had the rout to go over again I should bring no more baggage than could be conveniently carried in a pair of Saddle bags.

Love to all. The opportunity by which I send this will not allow me to write more.

AFFECTIONATELY, MY DEAR SISTER
Thy brother Fred Tyson

[Accompanying note]

Dear Sister I have taken the liberty of opening this, seeing Fred's writing. Harriette was well when I heard last and I hope to have her home on 7th day.[21]

With much love I remain
THY AFFECTIONATE BROTHER
James E. Tyson

[Accompanying cover note, in unidentified writing. Correspondence was shared between the Smith and Tyson families.]

When you write to Lizzie enclose this half who will *please return* my affectionate love to her and Richards, who asked to see the letters from JM

· · · · ·

On board Steamer *Panama*
Tuesday, August 1 1849

To Elizabeth Brooke Smith
DEAR LIZZIE

I wrote Thee from Panama the day before I left for San Francisco. I regret Fred did not leave with me, but as tickets are hard to procure here it was considered prudent for me to take advantage of the present chance and leave the other to provide and take care of the baggage, all of which I have left expecting Fred to bring it up on the *Oris* which we left at Panama and which we are told will sail about the 20th August.

It was a great trial to leave Fred and all my clothes that thee took so much trouble to prepair. I left Fred in charge of Doct. McMillan, a perfect Gentleman and said to be one of the most distinguished surgeons in the Army. He is a native of South Carolina but calls New Orleans his home. Fred and he room together. I have no fear of Fred's being unwell. He has stood the trip astonishingly and has grown very fat and has not been unwell since he left home. Most of the *Falcon's* passengers are left at Panama and nearly all on board have either left all or a portion behind.

I am getting along bravely and intend doing something in Sant Francisco till Fred comes up, then Ho for the diggings. The accounts from there still flattering.

WEDNESDAY NIGHT. After a hard day labour, for our boatmen having spent their time mostly poling instead of paddling with no great distance overcome, we arrived about 7 o'clock at a ranch filthy in the extreme, where I was refreshed with a cup of coffee and retired to my cuddy hole in the canoe where I rested fine.

THURSDAY. By 10 o'clock we made Gorgona,[22] where we were induced by the misrepresentations of Interested Individuals to take that route for Panama instead of continuing on up to Cruces. Those of our passengers who crossed from Cruces found the road much Better than the Gorgona route. The distance is said to be 21 miles from Gorgona to Panama. We travelled seventeen hours and spent one night on the road. Five miles out I lost my mule. The work was too much for him so Fred and myself took turns till unfortunately for us Fred's dobbin gave up about 7 miles from Panama, where two Individuals was to be seen nearly as good for nothing as their lost Horses, plodding on their way bound for California, a land they do not expect to reach without encountering some difficulty and deprivations. My feelings were almost inexpressible when nearly broken down and hungry, for we ate nothing from the time we left Gorgona expect a little green corn in an uncooked state. We were told we could get provisions on the road but we found it false. Coffee was all the natives would furnish us.

It was truly refreshing to a tired pair when about 4 o'clock on the evening of Friday the broad blue Pacific burst suddenly upon our vision. It was our first sight of it and under our feet at the distance of about a mile lay Panama, with nothing inviting to the weary travel-

Detail from *Incident on the Chagres River*, oil painting by Charles
Christian Nahl. Courtesy The Bancroft Library.

ler save the prospect of a few days rest. It has its ruins which are of interest but as my lot seems to be to see the Elephant,[23] I leave to Historians to describe and comment on the ancient greatness of this now dilapidated spot.

I [illegible] the miserable conduct—rather, fate—of our broke down mules. I have written before and told why Fred stopped and I pushed ahead. I wrote thee from Chagres, from Panama, from Acapulco, from Mazitsland, also two letters for Mother.[24] We did not land at Acapulco, merely stopping in to leave a mail. It was night when we entered the Harbour which by moon light is certainly a picture for a painter. We were 2½ days from Acapulco to San Blas, a once magnificient place beyond doubt, judging from its extensive ruins. It is now an insignificant mud village. From the large number of Quicksilver Flasks piled up, I should suppose it is to be a depot for the shipment of this article.[25]

The most remarkable incident occuring here in which I was interested was a purchase of what we thought was claret wine—two Boxes. We took it on the ship and next day opened it for a division when, lo, it turned out to be olive oil. I was fortunate enough to dispose of my portion at a profit sufficient to defray all the expense I had incurred on ship, being in demand amongst the passengers for dressing onions, which were the principal article of provision laid in at the above port. We spent some 5 hours and left about 6 in the afternoon for Mazitland, which we made next morning about 10 o'clock, being August 10/49. We were not permitted to land. While laying there the *California* came in, in 8 days from St. Francisco. Some of her passengers boarded us and gave us great encouragement. We left here the same day. From this point, I scribbled Mother and Lizzie a line which was sent per *California*.

I formed a favorable opinion of Mazitsland. It appears to be a place of some display of neatness. The houses appear of stone and covered with tile. The country around barren and dreary—from there to Cape St. Lucas like all we have seen—mountainous—broken—barren—dry.

AUGUST 11. The day after leaving Mazitsland we made this point— the extreme point of lower California where to our surprise we spoke the *Grey Eagle*, a ship you are familiar with. She was from St.

Francisco with 200 Mexicans bound home to Mazitsland from the diggings.

[The above incomplete letter-journal was written by JMS on the back of the following letter from an unidentified correspondent. Several lines are missing, possibly torn out by JMS to retain the sender's name and address.]

To Mr. J.M. Smith
DEAR SIR

Will you be kind enough on arrival at Chagres or Panama—as opportunity may deem, to drop me a line and give me your information as to transportation of frt. [freight] across the Isthmus—the cost, what kind or size of packages would be best, the rate of frt. from Panama to San F—etc. You can either write from Chagres or Panama, as the information you desire may enable you. I should be pleas'd to have an acct. of yr trip across the Isthmus, the difficulties to be guarded against in rainy weather and aught else that you think would prove of service to me. [portion missing] P.S. Please direct yr letter to this point and per first steamer.

• • • • •

Steamship *Panama*, August 6 1849

To Elizabeth Brooke Smith
DEAR LIZZIE

Owing to the kindness of Capt. Codman I am furnished with a place and implements for Penning a few lines. I am in hopes ere this Thee has rec'd a letter pencilled by Fred and myself from Panama. It is a source of great regret to me that Fred was left behind but he seemed to think it would be as well for him to wait and bring up the Baggage in the next steamer. I am in hopes ere this the *Unicorn* has arrived. She was looked for daily. Fred was in first rate health. I divided my money with him till he assured me he had enough, and left him with a Gentleman, Doct. McMilan, who assured me he would take care of Fred. I have no fear of Fred's getting sick. He has more prudence than you all give him credit for.

I cannot give at present an account of our trip over the Isthmus. My object now is more to relieve thy mind of any anxiety. I assure thee I am perfectly well, and if I had Fred and my Baggage would be as happy as a man can be who loves his home and those he has left behind him. As regards the prospects in California, I consider them cheering. I shall wait in St. Francisco till Fred comes up there. I think I shall strike for the diggings.

Lizzie, I think it will be as well for thee to subscribe to the *New York Tribune* as B. Taylor is with us and his letters will be published by Greeley.[26] He has promised to have one *Tribune* sent to thee. Thee would be amused to see what a life on the way to California is. I am in the steerage, but I can assure thee that as regards respectability, we can boast of as many fore as there are aft. We have Gentlemen with us who have ships out in St. Francisco, marching double file to the cook with their tin cup for coffee, and are feeding out of one Tub. Our fair [fare] is that of the sailors, but I take it for granted that all are, like myself, expected to encounter things a little rough, so I am favored with health. It is all I ask. Though provisions are coarse and rough, I have an appetite.

Kiss the little Boys. Remember me to all. Say I would write more, but I have not the Implements. I have not the place. This letter will be enclosed in one of Capt. Codmans and forwarded from Acapulco.

Dear Lizzie, Thee must excuse the rough manner in which my letters are and have been penned. But give me quiet and I am but a poor scribe but here, where all's hustle and confusions, I find the undertaking really arduous. People are talking and moving all round me and confuse me. I sent Mother a letter from Chagres which I take for granted she has rec'd. Do not let my absence trouble thee. I honestly believe it is for the best. I expect to be the owner of a first rate Farm near Jericho in less than two years. Adieu.

FROM THINE AFFECTIONATELY
John Marsh Smith

• • • • •

Steamer *Panama* off Magistland

August 10 1849

To Elizabeth Brooke Smith

DEAR LIZZIE

We have just discovered what we suppose to be the *California* bound down to Panama, by which opportunity I write. I am rejoiced to report myself well, strong and encouraged to go ahead. I am satisfied from all I can gather that California is the spot. I wrote thee from Panama and from Acapulco, in both of which letters I stated Fred has stopped behind for the baggage. I apprehend no sickness. The place is healthy, and Fred is in good hands. It was James advice to drive ahead, one or both. I shall look round and find something for Fred to do. He will be up nearly as soon as myself.

We left the *Oregon* at Panama when we left yesterday. We spent some 3 or 4 hours ashore at San Blas, a once magnificant old Spanish town now all delapidated, nought but ruins left, and in its stead mud huts covered with leaves, with a population of not more than 3 or 4 hundred.

Excuse the brevity. My object is to let thee know I am well. The order is just issued to stand by the gun. We are now going into the harbour of Magistland. It is about 10 in the morning of Friday August 10th.

Kiss the little boys. Give my love to all.

THINE

J M Smith

[Catherine Marsh Smith wrote the following on the previous letter from JMS.]

To Elizabeth Brooke Smith

Care [?] Matthew Smith

Baltimore, Md.

DEAR ELIZABETH

Thy letter was not sealed. I took the liberty to read it. I know thee will excuse a Mother's feelings. Hannah Ann is not improving as we could wish. She has never been able to be up to have her bed made, and Nurse was not able to Change her at all until the day before yesterday. She has constant head ache, some fever and a very sick stomache. Doctor Radle now thinks it is a gastric affection. She is able to sleep the fore part of the night and is quite relieved of her former disease. She fears much that her milk will leave her, but we are using all endeavors to prevent that. The Babe thrives with feeding and is very good. Hannah still keep her spirits. Were it not for that I should despair. I am in the midst of house cleaning. Painting, papering parlours, etc.

A letter from Cousins last evening says they will leave Nathans next fifth day, and calculated on being with us this day week.[27] We are trying, my dear E., to procure a dependable woman for thee, as Nurse for the dear Children. We thought we had one, and thy Father has just returned with a final refusal to go to the Country. She was highly recommended, and Father offered every inducement, said he would take her and her friend up, and if she did not like the appearance of things, would bring her immediately back. All to no effect, E. Anne has returned home. Thomas has gone to Boston on business.

Uncle T wants this for the cases.

THY MOTHER
CMS
[Catherine Marsh Smith]

• • • • •

San Francisco, September 21 1849

To John Marsh Smith
DEAR JOHN

I leave here in the morning too early to see you before I go, and I therefore leave this to say that when you leave Mormon Island to return to this place, you had better place in the hands of someone there a letter informing me of what you had done, to be delivered to me on my arrival there, should I go that route on my way back from Monterey, and advise me at sometime when you would return to Mormon Island in case you pursue the project of the Gold machine, in order that I may meet you there, and should an opportunity offer, write to me at Monterey.[28]

If the gold washing machine succeeds as Mr. Brinswade[?] describes it, William will join us with another one—and I recommend you to be on the look out for any speculation that promises great profit in any other way, and if I can I will join you in it.

Use every dispatch in your movements and get the work as quick as possible, and we may extend our operations together. I am confident there is a great field for profit in the interior of this country for an observant and intelligent young man and I know you will succeed in some other way if the machine fails. I have confidence however in Mr. Brinswade, and likewise his statements will be verified by your own when you return.

> With Best wishes for your success
> YOURS TRULY
> Jos. Hobson

Mr. Brinswade will give you a letter to his friends—ask him for it—and get William to give you one from Mr. Priest to his house at Sacramento City.

* * * * *

> *San Francisco,* September 22 1849

To Messrs McNulty & Stambaugh
Sacramento City
GENTLEMEN:

Allow us to introduce to your acquaintance Mr. J. Marsh Smith who leaves today for your part of the country.

Any attention to Mr. Smith will be considered a favor to us and will be gladly reciprocated at any time when in our power.

> In haste,
> YOURS VERY TRULY,
> R.H. Taylor & Co.

Regards to Mr. Hedrick

* * * * *

San Francisco, September 16 1849
[completed October 17, see below]

To William Talbott

DEAR WILLIAM

Owing to the unfortunate circumstance of not getting our baggage through from Gorgona to Panama in time for the steamer, it was deemed prudent on reflection by Fred and myself that I should drive on and make the Paradise, so discribed by the lively imagination and Golden Pen of a Freemont, an Emory, and a Bryant.[29]

Considering clothing as a matter not worth consideration, [and] Induced to believe that the clear canopy of our newly discovered *Italy* afforded all the covering requisite for the comfort and healthy protection to the Pilgrim on his expedition in search of the Golden Sands, my experience is soon given, for if I had not of borrowed an overcoat and blanket from a friend I would have frozen the first night. As regards the temperature of the climate, it is impossible to keep the run of it, the Thermometer flies up and down so fast, and when least expected, and its fogs, which prevail the greater part of the day, are so dense that you might hide behind them the inequities of the Administration of the now departed Jas. K. Polk....

Owing to many circumstances, the penning of the above was postponed. Tis now the 17 Oct, and I have returned from a tour of observation to Mormon Island where I went at the request of Jos. Hobson to see the working of a gold washing machine. Of some celebrity in these parts, he proposing to furnish capital to work it if I should report favourably. I am now waiting his return from Monterey, where he now is a member of the convention to form a state constitution.[30] I will send you a paper with proceedings up to this date.

I was quite pleased with the process of gold washing, but found without much observation that labour is the true capitel of this great and growing country, and such as can be procured at the place I was is of rather a worthless character, such as the floods of dissepation are scattering through the land to damn all water that is not half grog. When Joseph H returns I will give him a statement, and if he thinks well of the enterprise I will encamp for the winter amongst the mountains of California, and if a Bountiful Providence sees fit to favour me with health, I expect by the time the waters subside after the melting of the snows to come out *Jay Bird*. I am not afeard. There are other things in this country equally profitable and more civilized which I would prefer, but still, as my friend Joe furnishes the capital I will be influenced by his judgement.

You can say to Harry Warfield that I should like to see him, but to give up all idea of coming out. He could not be happy here. There are no comforts, and but few people who are not anxious to exchange their chances here of health for their homes and friends, whose voices are more cheering at the winter fireside than the crack of the rifle and the yelps of the wounded wolf with which the country abounds. I have not yet seen any other *varments*, and aint *anxious*.

There are an immense number of persons in San Francisco at this time, and there are not any but would like to be home. Gambling is the occupation of the masses. Tis disgustingly popular. This is an astonishing country. When a man buys a piece of property here he gets no guarantee deed, simply a receipt, and the way titles will be disputed here after a while will not be slow.

There are other places of importance besides San Francisco. Sacramento is a great place, about one hundred and fifty miles up the Sacramento river. Six months ago there was but one building. Now there are five or six hundred frames convered with canvass, and filled with men, women and children, familys of the imigrants from over the mountains, and I counted laying along the banks of the rivers at this town thirty sail of vessels, most of a large class: Ships, Barques, Brigs, Schooners, and Steam Boats. The shore is bold and large vessels lay so near its banks you can step on shore. The only Hotel is of frame, not as large as the tavern at Lavender Mill. It rents for Fifty thousand dollars a year. Grass grows in the low lands near this town in great abundance, but still it sells for six dollars per hundred pounds, and corn at this time four dollars per bushel. Still, teaming and carting is very profitable. Lawyers, Preachers, Doctors, Merchants are frequently found driving waggons and carts, and one man driving an ox team was pointed out to me as one of the Professors from Yale college.

You are aware Thos. Butler King of Georgia has been out here some time.[31] He resigned his seat in Congress and is selected as the candidate for Senator from this state. Of course, he goes opposed to slavery as this is unanimously a free state. Sailors and Negroes have never before seen such a country as this California. Big Oaks from little acorns grow. You know Steinberger was small after his troubles with the Western bank, but Phoenix-like he has risen from his ashes, and has become in this country a perfect Giraff, builds Hotels, buys lots, land, and has acquired for himself the title of the Baron. He entertains frequently and most extravagantly. He knows the ropes, and I predict time will a tale unfold.

I received a letter from Mother yesterday. Tell her I thank her for it. Was delighted to learn all well. I would write often, but it is difficult to find a quiet place. I have no quiet chamber to retreat to, to write. I am now stopping at Cross and Hobsons store on a table, consider it remarkably fine quarters. Have not slept on a bed since I left the steamer at Chagres.

> *Adieu.* Remember me to all.
> YOUR SINCERE FRIEND
> J. Marsh Smith

P.S. When I make money enough to live comfortable, and buy a little farm, I am away [from] here.

• • • • •

San Francisco, October 18 1849

To John Marsh Smith
Miner's Hotel
Puebla de San Jose
DEAR SIR

We have just received your favor of 17 instant and regret to learn that you did not meet with our Mr. J. Hobson.

If Mr. McDuffie should not be in San Jose on your receipt of this we request that you will proceed without delay to Monterey and carry out our instructions already given to you.

Mr. McDuffie offered to our Mr. Jos. Hobson in Monterey property there which the latter owned, and in case he proposes to give you the same at a valuation on which you can immediately realize half its price we wish you to take it—*but not if you can by any means do better, as we believe he is able to pay the full amounts.*

YOURS TRULY
Cross Hobson & Co

· · · · ·

Sacramento City, October 22 1849

To John Marsh Smith
DEAR JOHN

I recd yours on Saturday 20th and send Fred's letter this morning by an acquaintance of mine whom I can depend upon to deliver, and have also written myself. I have not heard from him since you left but if I do, will let you know, or rather will write to you and put in the post office. And this I believe is the last of letters in this country as far as Post Office is concerned. I hope you may select this place for business.

RESP YOUR OBT SERVT
James Lea[32]

· · · · ·

Mormon Island, October 23 [1849]

To John Marsh Smith
San Francisco, California
DEAR BRO

I have just recd your letter with our friend Jim Lea. I was sick for ten days after you left, but have never at any time been in want of funds and since my recovery have bought a first rate rocker and am more than paying expenses. Digging here pays about as well as when you left—from $5 to $20 per day on an average. I think you did well to let the large machine alone as the small companies who have purchased them are getting very tired of their bargains.

The gentleman who takes this letter down for me is about to leave.

AFFECTIONATELY YOUR BROTHER
Frederick Tyson

[Note on edge of envelope on the address side, apparently by JMS]

May 30 from JSH-10$ May 30th Loaned Fred dust 23.00

<u>cash 10.00</u>

33.00

•   •   •   •   •

San Francisco, October 30 1849

To Elizabeth Brooke Smith
care of Smith & Curlett
Baltimore, Md.
DEAR LIZZIE

Express to Mother my thanks for her kindness. Her favour up to August 14th I received. Thee was out of town. I trust Gilly's indisposition was not of a serious character. Dear little fellow. Do not recall to his memory the playfull moments I [used] to have with him. My absence I know does not torment little Tom,[33] and Lizzie, be happy. I came here but for one object, and I feel confident I will accomplish it, trusting I may be preserved in health and strength. I have not accomplished much yet, but I have had a good excuse to offer. The dysentarry has prevailed to a great extent since my arrival. I have been one of the afflicted. I would think myself well and go to work, but would render myself unfit for service the day after. I have been for three weeks in comfortable quarters and good service, and do feel thankful to report myself well. I weigh one hundred and forty nine pounds, being ten pounds more than I weighed when I left home.

I started with Fred on an expedition to Mormon Island proposed by Joseph Hobson. Was convinced the project he contemplated would prove unprofitable, and after recovering from a slight indisposition left Mormon Island to report as ordered by Joseph. Fred sent me word from there three days ago by no means to embark in the speculation, as the quicksilver machine was loosing cast amongst the miners.

On my return, I was embarked in a collection expedition to Monterey for Cross-Hobson, but met my man about six miles before I reached Monterey. He was on his way to St. Francisco so I was saved a ride on a mule that I was glad to dispense with. The roads through the country are magnificent, all as level as a floor though the country is very mountainous. I spent three days at St. Hosa the capital of the state of California.[34] (I shall not winter in the mines. I am to be engaged in a speculation that pays better and secures me a comfortable home.)

I shall use my efforts to keep Fred out of the mountains this winter. I could have secured for him two good situations had he been within reach: one 150 per month, one 240 pound [unexplained] per month. I have been engaged for some time as warehouse keeper for Cross-Hobson, and in a few days I expect to leave for Sacramento, Calif. on business. I will send for Fred and try and get him a situation. James Matthews slept with Fred a few nights since, reports him well. He has not yet averaged more than six dollars per day, but is quite sanguine of success.

When last in Sacramento, I stopped at a Hotel kept by James Lea, and the manner in which his house was kept reflected credit on him. Everything good, remarkably neat. Tom King has gone to the Southern Mines. He was well.

I have some gold of my digging in my tent at *Mormon Island* which I will get Fred to bring down. I came away and forgot it, so the amount is not large, but it is some.

Dear Lizzie, give my love to all at Jericho, all at home who enquire. Kiss the dear little boys and do not feel distressed about me. All is for the best. Excuse this confused mess as all is noise and bustle. There is no private places in California where a man can retire to write. Give my love to Han. I hope she is well, and the youngster. Tell Tony by no means to come out here at this time.[35] If I see anything I will send him word. He can come out and return home with Fred and myself when we return with our fortunes. Tell

Tony he would have to pay three dollars for a bath here. All are remarkably kind to me here. Captain, William and Joseph all requested to be remembered to you all.[36] Tell Thos. Marsh that Adamantine candles are worth here one dollar and fifty cents a pound, and scarce.[37] They sell the same here as Sperm. Soap here in abundance, about 3 to 4 cents per lb. Tell Robert and James drugs (dull).[38]

Tell James Tyson that in the last 10 days flour has gone from ten dollars to 22$. Such sales made today. Our supplies are principally from Chili. It does not do well to ship from the states.

I am waiting anxiously for the steamer with letters from thee. I cannot wait further as the mail closes tomorrow. Excuse all defects.

FROM THINE AFFECTIONATELY
John Marsh Smith

If on any occasion thee should not receive a letter from me by regular mail do not feel uneasy as there is great irregularity in the mails through this country. Remember me to *Curlett and Wm Talbot.*

· · · · ·

Sacramento City, November 20 1849

To Henry Tyson
Care of Tyson & Dungan
Baltimore, Md.
(favour of Mr. I. Lindsay of Boston)
DEAR HARRY

Enclosed you will find the *Placer Times* with nothing of importance save the ordinance laws & some election returns. Politics here are by the masses neglected and owing to that cause I fear, the transport of old Tamany will rule the roost in these parts, in other words the Politicians of this country appear to be New York *Locofocos.*[39]

I am quartered for the present at this place, Sac City, with a fair prospect of being able to realize some little dust this winter. I trust I may not be disappointed. Cheer Lizzie up. My consolation here is that I see thousands of men around me who have left all that was dear behind them for the present except in thought. I received Lizzy's letter with a lock of Gillie's and Tommy's hair. I hope Hannah Ann ere this is quite well. As Gillie and myself were such cronies, I some times fear my absence may distress him and if so tell them to mention my name in his presence as seldom as possible. I hope it will not be many months before I hail him at Jericho.

I regret to say, Fred is not well. The Doctor says he is by no means in a bad way. I shall take care of him if it takes every grain of dust I make. I have one of the best houses in the town, built of frame with a stove in the room and a cot for him to sleep on with plenty of Blankets. He has the fever of the country. I trust I have got through with my sickness. I had a long heat of it off and on. Now I feel well and weigh one hundred and fifty five pounds.

Say to Lizzie if she should not receive dates regularly from me not to be uneasy, as there is no mail from here to San Francisco than can be relyed on, sometimes not one in two weeks. Direct my letters as usual to Cross Hobson & Co, San Francisco. I have not yet rec'd any bill of lading of Fred and my things. Our little invoice will pay well.

If we had our house here at this time we could get over one thousand dollars for it. Such houses are renting here now for from three to four hundred dollars per month. Our cotton duck we could sell for 100 to 125¢ per yard. I will have to buy some myself and the least I can purchase for is one dollar per yard the bolt. Cornmeal is worth with us twenty dollars per [bushel] and we have two boxes Adamantines in our lot of Goods. We could sell every pound if we had them for two dollars per lb. Tell John Curlitt to look and weep, but such is a fact, that two hundred boxes of Adamantines would bring this day dust to the amt of ten thousand dollars. Flour has been high, what is called a Black Eye sold a few days ago at 50 dollars per bsl can now be bought for forty. A loaf of bread such as we buy at home for 6¼ ¢ I pay 62¢ for and at retail 62 a pound for good butter crackers. A few weeks ago things were different. It has not been 30 days since you could buy flour from 7 to 10 per list bbl. Beef is now selling for 50¢ per lb, such is the present state of affairs and there is not at this time one month's provision in the mines. Communication by team or pack generally cut off. Miners will have to foot it down if they want good grub. Some of them have lain in large lots of acorns, which are quite nutritious. For evidence of that fact, I refer you to Porkology or the fattening of swine.

Harry, I did once think myself romantic. I now have a chance of testing it, for I look from my window on the Sierra Nevadas covered with snow and this its valley knee deep in mud. I don't like either. I would like home and hope to fetch it before many months.

Tell Lizzy I would not that she should be here for all the Gold of the Mines. I can tell her some funny things when I get home. Tis strange to see all men and no woman. I think Jim Lea is going to make some money here. I saw on the street today Stillinger, Jimmy Keman's friend. Poor fellow looks bad. Say to Toney don't come to California. When I get home I will tell him all about it. The last great achievement is the navigating the Sacramento with steamers. The steamship *McKim* runs between San Francisco [and] this place, also the *Senator*, making three trips each week, with freight from San Francisco here 60¢ per foot on hundred pounds. There are some thirty large vessels lying along our River Bank, amongst them the *Baltimore, The Lady Adams* & *Sch. Ferdinand*, the one a brig the other a schooner. Mr. Dungan is going in business in this place, often has made some money.[40]

Not having ink that I can conveniently reach I write thee with pencil. Remember me to all.

Your Brother Affectionately
J. Marsh Smith

Tell my Mother when I receive a pile I will write her. That is all I am waiting for. Tell Toney to write me another letter. He gives me all the items.

A gentleman bound to the states promises to carry this so I enclose the paper. I know you don't mind expense.

• • • • •

Sacramento City, November 29 1849

To Elizabeth Brooke Smith
care of Matthew Smith
Sharp St. opposite Baptist Church
or Smith-Curlett
corner of Pleasant & Holliday Sts.
DEAR LIZZIE

Having an opportunity of sending by private hands, I take advantage of the chance. I have been very much engaged and even am so at this time. On my return to this place from San Francisco, I found Fred rather the worse of hard work and exposure, but luck has provided me with a comfortable house, where with my nursing and a good comfortable room I am happy to report Fred once more convalescent. He rode out today on horseback, has a good appetite but is careful to restrain it.

I am ashamed when I think of the time I have been in this country and not yet a single remittance. Like Fred, all I have made has gone for Doctor's fees, but I am once more and truly thankfull myself, and am not afraid but ere long the fruits of my labour may be presented to thy view.

I rec'd thy letter with a lock of our dear little boys hair. May a kind providence protect them. I hope I may realize enough to make them comfortable, for I never want them to feel as though California was their only chance. This is a wonderful country. Just to think, a community of men. I have not seen a half dozen or heard the voice of a single female, for the last five weeks. Those that are in the country have no comforts.

While I think of it, the letter thee wrote to me at N. Orleans I rec'd. It was forwarded from there by the proprietors of the St. Charles Hotel. I have not yet rec'd a Bill of Lading [for] our goods, yet shipped by Brother James.

A man told me he would give me for our house, delivered here, One Thousand dollars, but not having anything to show for it, we could not trade. Fred and myself expect to get even more than that amount for it. If I had here in this place one hundred boxes Smith & Curletts adamantines, I could sell them all for three dollars per pound. The price of washing is still six dollars per dozen. For beef I pay 50¢ per lb., 60¢ for 1 lb. loaf of Bread, Thirty-five cents a pound for white sugar, butter one dollar and fifty cents per lb., molasses 2 dollars to 2.50 per gallon.

I cannot advise Tony coming. It is merely on acct. of sickness, but if he is determined to come, let him cross the Isthmus and come direct to Sacramento from San Francisco. My home here is as comfortable as the nature of circumstance will allow. I have one of the best houses in town, but no private rooms. In one room I can sleep about seventy five, in the garret thirty, and on the office floor as many as consider it comfortable. If any one that thee may be acquainted with should be bringing a coloured servant, they must get a pass for him or her showing they are not runaways. If I had Mr. Thomas Williams here, I would be willing to pay him one hundred and fifty dollars per month.[41] I have two large oak trees back of my house, have made an offer of eight dollars per cord for cutting them into cord wood, but can't find anyone who is willing to work so cheap.

Tell Tony to send me newspapers direct to Cross Hobson & Co. We have no mail to this place though we have some thousand inhabitants. Remember me to my friends with love to all,

FROM THY AFFECTIONATE HUSBAND
J. Marsh Smith
Proprietor of the
North Fork & Yuba Hotel
for the present

P.S. Joseph Todhunter is with me.[42] I am very much pleased at his conduct and I do think he will continue firm in a pledge he made me before I took him. Fred is not employed at this time. It is advisable he should keep himself inside the house as much as possible during the bad weather. He seems to think when the spring opens he will make some money and I know he will. Tell Father and Mother to be easy about me. I trust providence may protect me and place me safe amongst you ere long.

THINE
JMS

This will be handed thee by a fellow traveller of mine and one that has been my friend, Chas. Ellis of N. York—excuse the rough condition of what I have penned. Kiss the little boys for me but do not speak of me to them. I am afraid it will set Gill to thinking which is not good for one of his build.

•　•　•　•　•

San Francisco, December 1849

To James B Bond[43]
Care of Brickhead-Pearce
Baltimore, Md.
DEAR JIM

Owing to the irregularity of the mails, your favour has not before reached me.

Yours being an important document, I write on its reception. I will forward this by private opportunity, will write you by mail. If you have 4 or 5 thousand dollars I say come by all means. With your knowledge of business, success is *sure*. Bring your money, *not* goods. I will not enter into particulars here for I have not time as I leave for Sacramento today, and I have no doubt but a letter by the regular mail will reach you as soon as this. Should this come to hand at an early date, say to Thomas that I am well. Have read Robt's letter but too late to operate, as the goods have been sold. The communications with the mines are cut off, and I do not think there is sufficient provision in the mines to last one month. There will be extreme suffering. California is no bubble—all, all, is reality. More in my next.

YOUR FRIEND
J. Marsh Smith

•　•　•　•　•

Sacramento City, December 26 1849

To Elizabeth Brooke Smith
Dear Lizzie

I rec'd per last steamer which arrived last month day of Oct 16th together with some back letters. I appreciate Roberts kindness but, like Captain Tobins Chicken that his literary friend swallowed, he spoke too late. I called for the goods he gave me an order for, but Winter & Latimer had bolted them. I should have been gratified beyond measure could I but have got them. I could have connected myself with a factor who had about an equal amt in cash, a man I know as a Gentleman, but such is life. Better luck next time.

In my last I told thee of a project Wm. Hobson & J. Wethered had in contemplation of getting up a Hotel in Sacramento.[44] They did not finish getting it up ere they made up their minds to dispose of the property, of which I am acting as sole monarch, but to no profit save the improvement of my health which thee sometimes says is worth more than money. I don't want thee to feel for me for I am going to make money and that honestly.

Everything is now in a state of *Status Quo,* Mud almost to a mule's back being one of the predominant features of the present state of the country. All communication with the mines is over for the present. Fred has entirely recovered from his illness, he bought a pair of Mules and waggon though there is nothing doing now. He makes Eight or Ten dollars per day clear after paying Three dollars per day for Horse feed. It is most wonderfull, with nothing but, [illegible] those that took the trouble to save hay which they got for the cutting and now are selling it at fifteen and sixteen cents per pound. Flour is now worth thirty five dollars per bbl., fresh beef fifty cents per pound, *sweet potatoes* sixty two cents per lb., Irish potatoes thirty cents per lb. *wholesale.* I have not yet rec'd a bill of lading for our House etc.

I have heard great news from the mines today, the high water has driven people to the hills where they never thought of digging and their success is great. When I think I can stand the Mountains, I may be tempted to give them a fair trial. A great deal of the land around and in town is now inundated. The general impression is that the water will not reach my ranch.

Tell Tony not to come out here. It would be impossible to draw a picture of its deprivations. Just think, a community of *Sea Critters* living in a land of mud and water. Tell Thos W. I wrote James Bond immediately on recept of his. I advise him to come and bring his money. There are now at this place laying some fifty Sail of large vessels and a population of about five thousand where twelve months ago there was not a Mark of Civilization. The Indians are scarce. Game plenty.

Dear Lizzie, I have made a good many friends but not much money. Don't fear. James Lea is well and doing a large business. He is proprietor of the Missouri Hotel. Joe Todhunter is staying with James Lea. He tells me he is to get 200 per month and his board. Fred tells me he is going down to San Francisco tomorrow, he says is financessing.

Dear Lizzie, give my love to all, Kiss the little boys for me. Hoping to see you all again. Happy, trusting I may be led in the right path. If owing to any circumstance thee should not hear from me don't feel uneasy, for if one gets into the country here he is where he hears nothing or can send nothing. Though Sacramento is so important a place we have no regular mail to San Francisco. Direct my letters as heretofore care of Cross Hobson. William Hobson is very kind to me and when in the United States I hope now he will have every attention from you all from

THY AFFECTIONATE HUSBAND
John Marsh Smith

p.s."The [Thy] Husband" alone so eligable was a sort of simultaneous lust of Eloquence as far as taste is concerned. I like "the [thy] affectionate," leaving out the "husband," as that is understood. I will leave it to the girls to decide.

JMS

Tell Father I rec his kind letter and will write him. I rec the Sum by Adams Exp.

JMS

The packages by the express are distributed near a bank before papers by the regular mail.

Notes to Chapter One

1. Frederick Tyson, who accompanied JMS, was one of Lizzie's younger brothers, born April 17 1828.
2. JMS was educated in Alexandria, Virginia, by Benjamin Hallowell, a leading Quaker, possibly the father of "young Hallowell."
3. Henry Tyson, another of Lizzie's brothers, born November 18 1820; Anne Tyson, a sister of Lizzie, born February 6 1825; Gilbert Tyson Smith, elder son of Lizzie and JMS, born April 30 1846; Hannah Smith Atkinson, a sister of JMS, born April 26 1821. Her husband, James, was in business in Baltimore with her brother, Thomas Marsh Smith.
4. A member of President Jackson's cabinet, in 1848 Cass had been the Democratic nominee for the U.S. Presidency, but was defeated by Zachary Taylor. Cass had supported the cause of "squatter sovereignty," the right of people in separate territories to determine the question of slavery for themselves.
5. A wooden side-wheel steamer of the United States Mail Steamship Company.
6. A "bile," or boil, was treated with a poultice of flaxseed, which JMS mentions in his next letter.
7. Chagres, a town on the river of the same name, was the Isthmus terminal of the United States Mail Steamship Company's New York run.
8. Built in 1837 at a cost of $800,000, the St. Charles Hotel was a New Orleans landmark, where planters going to the city to do business and engage in a little revelry usually stayed.
9. Catherine Marsh Smith, JMS's mother (1790-1870).
10. After publishing a highly successful account of his travels in Germany, in 1849 the *New York Tribune* commissioned Bayard Taylor (1825-1878) to record his impressions of the California gold rush. These were eventually compiled in Taylor's book *Eldorado*, excerpts from which are in the Appendix.
11. The Tyson family farm, about 25 miles from Baltimore.
12. Famous for his exploits in the Mexican war, Major John C. Hays was elected as San Francisco's first sheriff in 1849 and later became the U.S. surveyor general in California.
13. The *Orus*, a 250-ton steamer, was in commission in January 1849 from the mouth of the Chagres River to Cruces, a village where boatmen were usually paid and travelers transferred to land transport.
14. Among the health hazards of crossing the Isthmus were yellow fever, cholera, and ague, a malarial fever.

15. The Hobsons were social and business friends of the Tyson and Smith families. While the firm of Cross, Hobson was headed by Joseph Hobson, William was clearly the silent partner. In 1848 Joseph Hobson went to San Francisco on behalf of the firm with Alexander Cross; in 1849 he was elected as a delegate to the convention in San Jose to draw up a state constitution for California.

16. Thomas Marsh Smith (n.d.), a brother of JMS (see note 3 above); Thomas Marsh, JMS's maternal uncle; John Curlett, a partner of JMS's father, Matthew Smith; William Talbott, a close friend of JMS; Robert Tyson, Lizzie's youngest brother, born March 25 1830; James Tyson, Lizzie's oldest brother, born August 21 1816.

17. Situated south of Baltimore, between the branches of Lyons Creek and Herring Creek Bay, Jericho was evidently a property belonging to Lizzie's family.

18. The *Crescent City* was a side-wheel steamer on the New York-Panama run.

19. Harry Warfield was probably a Baltimore merchant who also served in Maryland's House of Representatives.

20. A sister ship of the Pacific Mail Steamship Company's *California* and *Oregon*.

21. Harriet S. Tyson was James Tyson's wife, and thus Lizzie's sister-in-law.

22. On the Isthmus.

23. To "see the Elephant" was an expression used to describe the California experience.

24. JMS spelled Mazatlan in several different ways.

25. Quicksilver, or mercury, was used in extracting gold and silver from mined ore.

26. Horace Greeley (1811-1872), a prominent abolitionist, founded the *New York Tribune* in 1841 and edited it until his death. The paper had a high moral and intellectual tone, and was dedicated to social reform and economic progress.

27. Lizzie's father, Nathan Tyson (1787-1867), was a leading member of Baltimore's Quaker community. He headed the firm of Tyson & Dungan, flour merchants, and served as first president of the Baltimore Corn and Flour Exchange.

28. Discovered by Mormons in 1848, Mormon Island was a low-lying, frequently flooded area of some seven acres on the South Fork of the American River. It was near Coloma and Sutter's Mill, where gold was found the same year. The area is now partially submerged by Lake Folsom.

29. John Charles Frémont (1813-1890), an explorer, mapmaker, soldier, and politician influential in California's early history; William Hemsley Emory (1811-1887), a soldier who, as a member of the Topiographical Engineers Corps, was involved in setting the United States' western boundaries between Canada and Mexico; William Cullen Bryant (1794-1878), editor of the New York *Evening Post* for 50 years, and poet.
30. California's State Legislature met in San Jose in 1849.
31. A former U.S. congressman, in 1849 Thomas Butler King was President Taylor's adviser on California statehood. Although he was too ill to attend the San Jose convention, he reported the proceedings in detail to the secretary of state. In 1851 he was appointed collector of the Port of San Francisco.
32. James Lea was proprietor of the Missouri Hotel in Sacramento. JMS does not tell Lizzie that the hotel, on J Street between 2nd and 3rd, was also one of Sacramento's outstanding gambling halls.
33. Thomas Marsh Smith, JMS's younger son, born January 28 1848.
34. San Jose, California's first city, founded in 1777.
35. Anthony M. Smith, a younger brother of JMS, born May 29 1826.
36. Captain James Hobson of the *Iona* was a brother of William and Joseph Hobson.
37. Adamantine candles: The trade name for long-burning candles made from six pounds of tallow, two ounces of camphor, four ounces of beeswax, and two ounces of alum.
38. "Drugs" refers to linseed and tung oils, candles and related hardware, items sold by the firms of Smith & Curlett and Smith & Atkinson.
39. A radical faction of the Democratic party in New York, organized in 1835 in opposition to banking interests and monopolies.
40. Most likely a relative of Nathan Tyson's partner.
41. Thomas Williams was probably a family employee. According to Judge Clark, there is a family legend that Matthew Smith, father of JMS, settled in Baltimore rather than farther south because his bride, Catherine Marsh, said she "could never marry a slave owner."
42. Joseph Todhunter was eventually employed by James Lea at the Missouri Hotel.
43. J.B. Bond, a friend of JMS, of Brickhead-Pearce, Baltimore.
44. J. (Jas.) Wethered appears to have been an older relative of the John Wethered who figures in Anthony Smith's letter of April 30 1850, and in JMS's letters of June 28 1850 ff.

CHAPTER TWO
1850

. . . . .

San Fran[cis]co, January 7 1850

To John Marsh Smith
DEAR JOHN

It may be agreable to you to hear from one who has lately seen your family—on the 6th of Nov'r they were all well and had received acc of you shortly before.

We are here almost up to our knees in mud, and business very dull, all however are looking for better times in a couple of months. So you refused to make money by encouraging gambling! I can't tell you how glad I was to hear it—to know that there was one at least of our old friends who had the courage to hold on to moral principle in spite of pecuniary disadvantage. I think just as you do on the subject—let us both persevere as *you* have commenced, & if we do not make as much money as others we shall feel that the blessing of God is upon what we may gain & can, when we return home, enjoy our means with Clear Consciences & without being ashamed to look our old friends in the face.

I have not "set up my Shingle" yet, but shall do so before long in the "common Line." Let me hear from you.

YR. FRIEND
JB Bond[1]

Is there a chance to make money [in] Sacram[ento] by "lots" now— or is it over done? Write to me if you see a bargain—& also generally in business matters when you have time.

• • • • •

Sacramento City, January 20 1850

To Nathan Tyson
DEAR FATHER[2]

This is the first time I have addressed Thee. I assure Thee it was not for want of inclination nor was Thee forgotten. That is impossible. Home and dear Friends are ever present to my thoughts. I have been delaying, trusting Fortune might favour me and I be able to give some good account of myself.

Ere this through Lizzie Thee has probably learned that fate led and disease compelled me to resort for a subsistance and wholesome shelter to an occupation not in accordance with Thy, my Fathers, or my own views or inclinations. On my arrival in this country I had much to contend against, having left Fred in Panama, the grave land of the Isthmus emigration. I felt anxious for his safe arrival and without a change of clothing, I felt restrained from appearing amongst those who might have favoured me. I did not remain idle. I applied myself and that hard. I will not tell you at what, it will do to laugh over if a kind Providence sees fit to restore me in your midst.

My Friends left for the mines, with them my spirits went and sickness soon followed. When Fred arrived I had grown better, and had a proposition made me by Joseph Hobson to enter into a mining operation, which would have been attended with considerable expense if undertaken and which would, as I reported after making my observations, have proved a failure as it has with all that have undertaken it. I feel in this instance satisfied with my judgement and rejoiced at my escape for those who enjoyed a like enterprise have been unsuccessful.

In the meantime, William H. and Jas. [torn segment] Wethered purchased a property in this city and proposed that they should fit up the house and give it to me on mutual acct. Nothing else offering and a prospect of a long and wet winter, and not able to stand the exposure of the mountain snows in the condition I was at the time, I thought it better to take hold. I did so. In the meantime, they, Wm H [and] J W, relinquished the Idea of carrying out Their contemplated plan and have appointed me their agent to dispose of the property for which they want Fifteen Thousand dollars cash. It may seem singular to Thee, but for this property they ask as a rent one Thousand dollars per month—have been offered over seven hundred per month. The business has not paid me but tis more than a compromise. I have regained my health and honestly believe that the good comfortable quarters it afforded Fred in as severe a spell of illness as has ever been his lot, is now the cause of his restoration to health and strength.

Fred left here some two weeks hence for San Francisco. I have not heard from him, have learned of the arrival of our little Invoice and take it for granted Fred is giving it his attention as he promised to do so. He is quite fortunate in being out of this miserable place at this time, for ten days past all is one vast Ocean and I feel as though I were at sea, the snow capt Sierra Nevada the only land visible from my second story window. Water in front of my house when at its height was *SIX FEET* and four feet on first floor. Hundreds are ruined but none complain. *The cry is Ho for the mines.*

I saw today a man that drives a Team for Fred and was rejoiced to learn from him that Fred's mules had been saved. The loss in stock has been great and the prospect is it will be very high in the spring. The mountains are now covered with snow and when the spring thaws come we *expect a flood.* We live on Salt Pork and drink the water of the streets. The anticipation of another flood has completely unsettled our community and many who have amassed means now feel their distress and poverty, talk cheerfully of drawing on the Mountain Banks for help and many are prepairing to leave for the mines. It is the general impression nothing will be done here for a couple of months.

The idea of remaining inactive for so long and the proposition from many to join them and recollecting Thy encouraging advice to give the mines a fair trial has induced me to think seriously of it. I intend going down to San Francisco in a few days if I can raise the means I want. I can do well Teaming freights to some of the nearest mines where you can with oxen make a load a week. Rate of freight is fifty cents per pound or fifty dollars per hundred.

I have not received any letters by the last Two steamers but take it for granted there are some for me in San Francisco. I was engaged writing to Lizzie when I was informed of the rise in the river. In the hustle that ensued it was lost but will try and write to forward by the same conveyance that takes this. I wish Thee and dear Lizzie and all interested so deeply in my welfare may be of good cheer. I feel great confidence in my ultimate success. I can acquire money. All I ask is health which I trust a kind Providence may see fit to bless me with. I feel as happy as most Californians who have as much to endear them to those so dear but absent. My ideas are, should I start for the mines, to remain there till the sickley months approach. The account from the mines are encouraging.

Jas Lee has suffered severely from flood. None have escaped loss. Flour we pay for a single barrel at this place forty dollars per barrel. I understand it can be bought in San Francisco for fifteen dollars. Barley I saw sell at auction the day before the flood at Fifteen cents per pound, Ten Bags, with the priviledge of One Hundred. They are retailing it at the Fort Sutters, the nearest dry land to us, at thirty cents per pound used entirely for feeding horses, mules.[3]

I am really delighted to learn from Lizzie's letters that Thee and Gillie are such devoted friends. I anticipate a great deal of pleasure from the company of the Little Boys should we all be spared to meet. Lizzie gives me most glowing accounts of Tommy's progress. Say to her I shall leave this country with all possible dispatch when I can show myself amongst you as a man. With love to you all and affectionately to Lizzie and the litle Boys' Grand Mother Ellicott and my Father and Mother Smith and all the rest.[4]

P.S. do not feel uneasy about me. Every body treats me kindly and I have made many friends but I know the way to retain them is not to use them so I rely entirely on my own application.

THY AFFECTIONATE SON
J. Marsh Smith

IN ITS ISSUE of January 5 1850, the Sacramento *Placer Times* notes the lovely weather and the receding water from the melting snows. Then, on January 15, an "extra" reported the onslaught of extremely high south, southeasterly winds and driving rain. Within five days waters from the rising river and rains were filling the slough on I Street between 1st and 3rd, rising to 2nd and 3rd streets by nightfall. By Thursday, January 18, according to the newspaper, the entire city of Sacramento "within a mile of the Embarcadero was under water with the exception of a few high points on the bank and on 10th Street. Almost all houses had water on their first floors, many swept away.... There is a great loss of provisions and goods. Many have lost 40 to 50 yoke of cattle, great numbers of horses and mules." Miraculously, only one person was drowned (swept from the deck of a boat). One end of a new two-story brick building collapsed. Sutter's Fort, on high land, accommodated patients evacuated from the hospital. A mile inland from the Embarcadero, where the land rose 10 to 20 feet, a tent city sprang up as shelter for refugees.

It was the worst flood since at least 30 years previously, when Sacramento had been little more than a small settlement at the confluence of the Sacramento and American rivers. Within a week the waters had receded to below the Embarcadero. The City Council, in almost continuous session, had raised funds for the Hospital and was considering plans for a river embankment. The *Placer Times* expressed hope that another week would find things "back to normal." Meanwhile, enterprising citizens panned the waters for gold with some success, and hopes rose that the floods had uncovered more lucrative areas in the hills.

Detail from the print *View of Sacramento City* as it appeared during the great inundation in January 1850. Courtesy The Bancroft Library.

On January 26, the newspaper reported that "walking is a little soft," and there was another brief but intense storm with a "howling southeasterly" and rains. The post office reopened. Since it was a fairly sturdy building, "people [were] able to get their letters without standing knee deep in mud."

• • • • •

Sacramento City, January 22 1850

To Elizabeth Brooke Smith
DEAR LIZZIE

I have written a few lines to Father Tyson and will envelope this in the same package. I shall not at present give Thee a lengthy epistle. In the letter to Father, I gave an acc't of the flood. It is now subsiding but no one anticipates business for a couple of months. People of our city, the *Amphibian City,* a great many are leaving for the mines. The news from high up on the Yuba is great so that many who have engaged in business here are preparing to leave to dig. I expect to leave for the Yuba [River] about the first to middle of February. I expect to have plenty of Company. Will write Thee before leaving and rejoiced to learn of your all being well and do not give yourself any uneasiness about Fred and my-self.

I want thee dear Lizzie to write me regular and direct as usual to Cross Hobson & Co and do not feel uneasy at not hearing from me if such should be the case. I expect to remain in the mountains till June if I keep well, which I have no doubt I will be able to do. There is no prospect of starvation in this country, plenty of provision every where. I write this in a hurry, will write in a few days. Dear Lizzie keep your spirits up, I am not a *feared*. Kiss the little boys. Thine affectionate.

J M Smith

Say to *Toney* that he would not like this country and do not come out, you must not believe one half of what you hear from him through the Public Prints.

• • • • •

Congress authorized mail service to the Pacific Coast in March 1847, and mail contracts the following year provided subsidies to the United States Mail and the Pacific Mail steamship lines. However, with the discovery of gold and the enormous profit to be made in the passenger business, both companies seem to have developed a certain ambivalence. Carrying passengers was given precedence over delivering mail, as R.T.P. Allen, special agent for California and Oregon, observed in May 1849. In a letter from Panama to the U.S. postmaster, he wrote: "I observe a tendency on the Atlantic side to make the mail service a secondary matter, and to *run for passengers*. This needs correction..." [Frickstad]. In February 1850, George Swain, prospecting for gold in California, wrote: "...no mail; that must come by the *Falcon* [The United States Mail's flagship], which the Government with admirable ingenuity, contrives to have always arriving behind private enterprise.... Our big men in Washington don't know or care much about mail, if office and pay can be secured, apparently..." [Holliday].

The regular run from New York to Chagres took from nine to eleven days, but the fleet was inadequate for the increasing amount of mail, and transport across the Isthmus was haphazard, relying as it did on local portage by dugout canoe and mule. It is not surprising that JMS repeatedly asked for his correspondence to be directed to Cross, Hobson in San Francisco, and that he and others out west seized every opportunity to send letters home with friends and acquaintances returning east.

On January 19 1850, the Sacramento *Placer Times* commented: "The Post Office: This interesting concern has been closed nearly two weeks, government having made no provision for paying clerks, and the Postmaster being in a quandry [sic] whether to go to work on his own hook or not. The post office as conducted heretofore is wholley [sic] inadequate to the wants of the community, and it may as well be closed as kept open. Private enteprise has rendered that shabby affair quite unnecessary."

In light of the situation, it is remarkable that the gold dust JMS enclosed in a letter of 1850 was safely delivered to Lizzie, and that by as early as 1851 letters to people in Oregon City were listed in the local newspaper for collection at the post office. The letters may have taken at least two months to get there, but get there they generally did.

Post Office, corner of Pine and Clay streets, San Francisco, illustration from *Annals of San Francisco*, 1855. Courtesy The Bancroft Library.

· · · · ·

Sacramento City, February 16 1850

To Elizabeth Brooke Smith
Dear Lizzie

I recv'd a few days ago thy favour of Dec 8th also one from Mother & one from John Curletts, all I assure thee truly acceptable. Yesterday I recvd a letter from James containing Bills of Lading dated some time in August, also a very pleasant one from Harriet. Say to Harriet Had I recvd it in time I should have written her. I will write her from the mines. Is it not a miserable state of affair that we should be so neglected by the general government, letters written and posted in August just coming to hand in February.

The goods shipped have been recvd.

Fred is in San Francisco in charge of them. He has put the House up and rented the lower room at one hundred and fifty dollars per month. Several of my friends from San Francisco just arrived report Fred as being very well and very stout.

Day after tomorrow I anticipate starting for the Georgetown ore diggings.[5] My partner for the mines is an Ohio man, a merry fine stout, decent fellow, his name is High.[6] We are to be joined in a week by one or two Oregon men. I am accompanied by my friends from San Francisco. We have two doctors in the party, one a South Carolina man who came out in the *Falcon* with me. The other an Englishman and gentleman. The others are a Mister Jakes from South Carolina, one a Yankee by the name of Porter, a young man by the name of Scott from Richmond,[7] he a brother of Geo. T. [illegible] and two young men, one from Baltimore named Williams, a son of a Mr. Williams, Bookeeper for Harry Carson & Cox, The other of the same name a cousin of the former, a pleasant and very agreeable company. We pay only five cents per pound freight and allow ourselves about fifty pounds each. The reports from the mines is good. George Town is on a stream that emptys into the middle fork of the American between the Middle of the North and Middle and about seventy five miles from Sacramento City. It was our intention to strike direct for the North but there are such numbers going there that we have considered it prudent to go where we will be more secluded. The snow at the Yuba mines is very heavy and at George Town it has nearly disappeared.

I don't want thee to feel any uneasiness about me. I get along first rate and am not without hope of success. Say to Mother if I do not write her in the morning she and Father should have a letter from the diggings. Say to Mother that. Say to Mother the only varmits here that trouble us are fleas of an enormous size, if they don't bite a fellow over at night they make him roll. My love to all. Kiss the dear little boys and tell them all to be good and mind what Thee tells them. I wrote Father Tyson by last steamer.

FROM THINE AFFECTIONATE
J Marsh Smith

DEAR FATHER AND MOTHER

I owe both of you a letter each and hope shortly to be able to give you one from some rich diggings. I leave in the morning God willing and no preventations. There are nine of us in the company, all pleasant orderly men, and am in great good spirits at having fallen in with them as I thought a few days since my party would have been composed of but one or two. We have two good doctors in the Company. I hope Providence may favour us [with] health. I want Mother to believe but little she hears of this Country. It is a peaceable country. San Francisco is a noisy place. I have not seen a Poisonous Snake since I have been in this country. Fleas bother as our greatest terror in this wilderness. You must not despair of my success, I have not. I will take first opportunity to appear amongst you when I can come right. I have got accustomed to do without comfort and there is no chance of starving. Give my love to all and remember me to Wm. Talbott. If cousin Marshes are in town say I have not forgotten them.

YOUR AFFECTIONATE SON
J. Marsh Smith

· · · · ·

Some Where in the Mountains, February 28 1850
[Seal of] Sacramento March 18 1850

To Elizabeth Brooke Smith
Care of Smith & Curlett
Baltimore, Maryland
DEAR LIZZIE

Hearing of an opportunity to forward a letter to Sacramento City, and not knowing when another may occur, I take advantage of the present. Am truly thankful Happy and rejoiced to report myself in first rate Health and Spirits. The happiness I anticipate should a kind providence see fit once more to restore me to Thee, our little ones, and dear friends and home is of a character beyond expression. I am happy and comparatively light hearted here in this Wilderness. I hope through a spirit of true thankfullness that I am well and every day feel stronger and more able to contend with the inconveniences and might say deprivations which the life I am leading necessarily incurs.

I am now encamped with a party of twelve including myself about eighty miles above Sacramento City, where the face of white man was unknown til last summer, and feel as free from harm as though I were at Osceola. Don't let tales of California life torment Thee. Most are mere fabrications. In the midst of [a] newly discovered Gold Region we are compelled to remain inactive for the present during the heavy snows that have fallen since our arrival. Our time is mostly spent at this time in attending to our comforts such as rolling logs and keeping most magnificant camp fires burning, Such as Thy Father, mine, and Uncle Thomas would delight to sit by. We have our tents pinned as close down as possible so that no air can get under them and then our magnificant fires as close as is safe. Though the nights are cold we lay huddled up close together with a plenty of Blankets and our feet to the fire sleep soundly and undisturbed.

Dear Lizzie, I never retire without thinking of Thee and the little Boys and the happy hour when I may be restored to you which I trust is not far distant. May it so please a kind providence to grant so great a favour. As soon as the weather gets so we can operate I

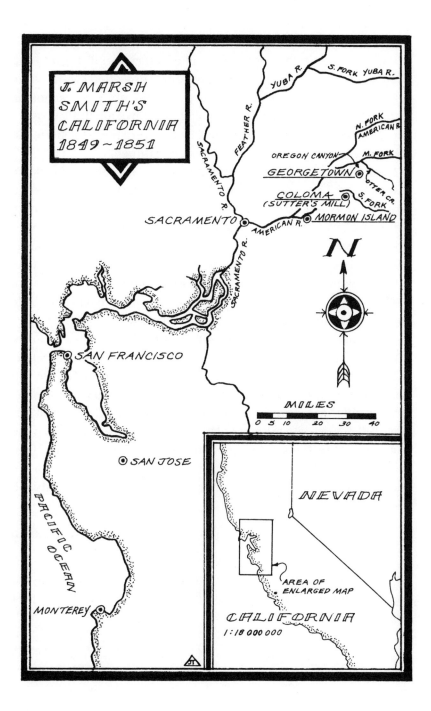

J. MARSH SMITH'S CALIFORNIA 1849~1851

S. FORK YUBA R.

YUBA R.

FEATHER R.

N. FORK AMERICAN R.

OREGON CANYON

M. FORK

GEORGETOWN

SACRAMENTO R.

COLOMA
(SUTTER'S MILL)

OTTER CR.

S. FORK

SACRAMENTO

AMERICAN R.

MORMON ISLAND

SACRAMENTO R.

N

MILES
0 5 10 20 30 40

SAN FRANCISCO

SAN JOSE

NEVADA

PACIFIC OCEAN

AREA OF
ENLARGED MAP

MONTEREY

CALIFORNIA
1:18 000 000

intend applying myself with all my energys. Success in mining is not always certain, it is very much of a lottery, but if it is a losing game it is by no means a disreputable one. Some men realize large amounts, thousands suffer, but why should my chance not be amongst the successful. I am not going to believe anything else til I am convinced by actual experience. Our party expects to operate in the Oregon Canyon where we are now encamped.[8]

Dear Lizzie, I am now amongst the tall pines Freemont speaks so glowingly of. They are truly gigantic trees. We have one of rather an ordinary size against which our fire is built, which is four feet in diameter. I would willingly exchange it for a well, puny but well stocked Peach or Apple tree. Thee must feel perfectly easy about I have plenty to eat, plenty of warm Bed clothing, and no scarcity of fire wood and a pleasant set of companions and the consolation of having in our party two married men who have wives and little ones. It is an old saying, misery loves company.

I have not seen Fred for some weeks. I enclose a letter received since I left Sacramento City. I will try and raise ink so as to direct my letters. Write me and direct as usual to Cross, Hobson & Co. We will send down in a couple of months for letters so keep me posted. Write by all the steamers. I recd a letter written by Harriet last August. Tell her to write me and tell me all the news. Tell Tony to write and give me the items. I want to write Thomas Marsh & Father. I am saving myself till I get to making the big pulls. Give my love to Rebecca & Robert, Fathers and Mothers, Sisters, Brothers, Friends and Kiss the little boys.

FROM THY AFFECTIONATE HUSBAND
J. Marsh Smith

When an opportunity offers I will write Thee. Do not feel uneasy at any delay for it is hard to get letters taken from here to the post offices.

THINE
JMS

• • • • •

Sacramento City, February 20 [1850]

To John Marsh Smith
Georgetown diggins
DEAR BRO

I arrived this morning. Charlie Todhunter and myself are going into teaming business in this place. My house in San Francisco is finished and the lower floor rented for 150 per month. I have just seen High who is going up in few minutes and I must conclude, no news stirring. Steamer not yet arrived. Hoping, my dear Brother you will succeed well in your mining operations.

> AFFECTIONATELY YOURS
> Frederic Tyson

My best respects to the Messrs Williams. Please write and let me know how you are getting on.

· · · · ·

> *Otter Creek,* 6 days above Sacramento
> near the Middle Fork of the American
> April 2 1850

To Elizabeth Brooke Smith
DEAR LIZZIE

It is with extreme delight I take advantage of an opportunity which, although it deprives me of two companions I regret to part with, offers a Medium by Means of which I can forward to thee a few lines which I know will be ever so acceptable. I look forward with the fondest hope to the day of My return, but feel no uneasiness about Me. I am carefull of My health and person and trust to God to guide me.

I left Sacramento as thee will see by the Diary* if it so may be called. Thee will see by refering that owing to great number of

---

* JMS's diary follows. JMS enclosed the portion up to, and including, March 28 in his letter to Lizzie of April 2.

Snowy & Rainy days we have had but little labour in comparison to what would have been done Weather permitting. I intend to remain in the mines till the last of June if My health continues so good as it is now.

My last dates from home are one from Thee of Dec 2nd and the 10th from Mother. I anticipate a pile of acceptable letters and papers when I get to San Francisco. I regret I did not see Fred before I left Sacramento. He returned there a day or two after I left. I make two packages of my letters to Thee. In this I enclose 15 small pieces of gold dug by Myself on Otter Creek weighing about 1/2 ounce and about 1/2 ounce of fine Gold dug by Fred and myself at Mormon Island last fall. I would send more but its an experiment sending by mail.

Dear Lizzie, Kiss the Dear little boys for Me. Remember me to All, all most kindly. I will write Thee by every opportunity that offers. Feel no uneasiness. I intend writing to Mother and Father. Excuse my brevity, but I have done a hard days labour and want to write as many letters as I can as opportunity to forward them dont often offer.

FROM THY AFFECTIONATE HUSBAND
J. Marsh Smith

I regret I have not ink to marke the little Bag of Gold I send thee. I know it would be safest for if this letter opened the [letterfold] it is in [letterfold] 1 inch wide [illegible]

[Enclosed in letter to Lizzie]

Otter Creek, 6 days above Sacramento
near the Middle Fork of the American
[April 2 1850]

To Matthew Smith and Catherine Marsh Smith
DEAR MOTHER & FATHER

Five of our party having become rather discouraged made up their minds today to leave for more Civilized parts, giving a chance to write and forward by them to San Francisco. The last dates from home is Mothers of the 16th December. You must excuse non recpt from me as this is the first chance to forward I have had since being in the mines.

Mother states the Horrible accounts she heard of Bears, reptiles, Indians, etc, all of which are Fabricating. I turn into my blankets after the labours of the day and sleep as soundly and enjoy my repose as unconcerned as any one who has nothing to fear, trusting that the same God who has watched over me this far may see fit to deliver me safe amongst you again.

I have written dear Lizzie and sent her a kind of diary. I have been working hard today and feel weary. On looking up I find my candle is fast dwindling. I enclosed Lizzie a specimen of my diggings. It was my intention to write John Curlett, Thos. M, Robert & James, William Talbot, Uncle Thomas and send each a specimen of the like kind but I am too tired. The candle I am writing by is a mould tallow. They cost near four dollars per pound.

Mother was anxious to know what we feed on at the mines. Enclosed she will find our bill of fare. There are four in our mess. Pork & flour is the song. We get fat on it.

The waters at present are too High for profitable mining. The Snows melting on the mountains that surround us in the valley here, all is delightful. I would like to send you some of the magnificant Flowers which we trample under foot. Excuse the brevity of this, it is more to show you are remembered by

YOUR AFFECTIONATE SON
J. Marsh Smith

Some day if I can raise ink I will write you a letter. Give my love to all.

It was my intention to have stopped work early this afternoon, but having felled a large Pine Tree for the purpose of building a dam to drain the main stream it took a notion to fall just where we did not want it, and laboured late to get it in its place, so I left writing too late to accomplish what my inclinations would stimulate me to do, but being now in the way of my friends who wish to retire I am necessarily compelled to knock off.

YOUR SON AFFECTIONATELY
JMS

I am going to give the mines a fair trial and if by the last of June I have a capital I shall go to San Francisco and by trading a man here with money cant well help rapidly increasing it. I am doing as well I think as any of the miners about these diggings. You must not feel uneasy or troubled about me. I shall leave California with all dispatch when I get my pile.

JMS

• • • • •

[Pencilled across right-hand corner]
April 2nd 1850 Enclose in a letter of date of April 2nd Lizzie 1 ounce

FEBRUARY 17 1850. This day at 2 o'clock left Sacramento City in small company with Doc't Wright of England, Tom Williams of Baltimore, Bill Williams of Arkansas and [missing] Scott of Richmond, Va. Old Jim Foley of Missouri, teamster. Our freight consisted of Blanketts, Gold washers, Picks, Pans, Spades, pickles, Beans, Tea and Coffee, destination Georgetown. Made at 6 o'clock of same day what is known in these parts as the nine mile house.[9] This house is about the outscurts of Civilization. No California settlements beyond this. All is wilderness save where the Yankee has stuck along the trail his log cabin trading post. The nine mile house being crowded so that after a California supper for which we paid one dollar and fifty cents and warming our heels, we spread our blanketts on the ground in a tent we found unoccupyed and slept till we were aroused to breakfast on the morning of the 18th. It rained quite hard during the night but did not inconvenience us.

FEBRUARY 18. We are all well, day delightful, road good. This afternoon arrived at Morman Island, the first or nearest digging yet discovered to Sacramento City. This is a beautiful place and reminds me of the scenery around Ellicotts Mills.[10] My ill success here last fall, my sickness, Fred's illness, and a prominent and well stocked graveyard rendered it rather odious to me. This place, I came to it last fall a miner and left it Minus. Such cases are not rare in this great and growing country. I found considerable improvement here and the diggers doing as well as they did in the fall. After supper we made inquiry to know if we could lodge in the house on the dirt floor. Being accommodating, they allowed us the priviledge on consideration on our paying fifty cents each. The Landlord, his wife and children took the bed. My place was by the side of it on the floor. Old Jim Foley at the Bottom, and the rest circling around with our feet to a first rate fire. Slept first rate.

Aroused in the morning to the Cook walking over us. We soon breakfasted and at 8 o'clock on the morning of Wednesday 19th, passed through a beautiful country valley and mountains, timber oak. Our wagon mired and we were compelled to pack on our backs about two hundred yards through a swamp and work out the empty wagon. All in good spirits and well. Made the day about fifteen miles and stopped at night at a tavern on Beaver Creek where the land-lord done all in his power to make us comfortable. He was evidently a gentleman at home and used to a different life from the one he was leading. As a mark of my high esteem I presented him with a Brass Breast pin which cost me at home 12½ cents. In return he gave me a Brass Ring set with something like diamonds and Valued at about the same price. It was a custom with him to give a cigar instead of desert after meals, being short of one and having plenty of the other. It rained from four o'clock on the 19th and continued a greater part of the night and there are diggings at Beaver Creek. The gold is 22 Carats fine.

FEBRUARY 20. Laid up till about 12 o'clock in hopes it would clear but, despairing, started in the rain and made about ten miles mak-ing this day Coloma or the Mill. This is the place where gold was first discovered about 18 months since. It is a beautiful spot in a Valley of the mountains. This mill was located here on acc't of the Timber being pines of most noble dimensions. Here we had com-fortable accomodations and walked down to take a look at the cele-brated race.

FRIDAY, FEBRUARY 22. We left Coloma early in the morning with a tedious march up an abrupt mountain said to be 3 miles to the sum-mit, which we reached at 2 o'clock. There was to be a Ball here at night, admission one ounce. We made this day about 10 miles and encamped at night in our tents on the snow and distant about 6 miles from Geo. Town. We are all well.

SATURDAY, FEBRUARY 23. Made Geo Town about 12 o'clock.

Cleared the snow, built large camp fires to dry the ground, and pitched our tents under some of the most magnificant pines this world can produce. The country beyond this being so broken, we make this our camping ground till we prospect and find good diggings. Snow about 6 inches deep.

SUNDAY, FEBRUARY 24. Was spent as a day of rest, watching the camp fires and preparing our meals.

MONDAY, FEBRUARY 25. Started out with a party of some six and tried prospecting. Sunk several holes to the depth of six feet, but the water run in on us, so we could accomplish nothing. At five o'clock commenced snowing, raining, and hailing, blowing in, which lasted all night. Prepared our coffee and hard bed and turned in for the night. We kept dry and I slept most delightfully.

TUESDAY, FEBRUARY 26. Snowed till 11 o'clock, cleared up, and was pleasant. Stayed in camp during the day, the snow being too deep to accomplish anything.

WEDNESDAY, FEBRUARY 27. Moved all day. Two of our party went out hunting, returned unsuccessful, the heavy snow having driven the Game down on the lowlands and in the Valleys. They heard a report of some Indians having attacked a camp some five miles from us and wounding one or two. The Indians were pursued, the result I did not learn. Poor fellows seldom escape after an adventure of a hostile character. This day being so very bad and uncomfortable, found it difficult to keep up fires. Three of us concluded to go and spend part of the day at a tavern for the sake of a good stove and tolerable dinner, for which we paid 2$ each. At night returned to camp and slept comfortably.

THURSDAY, FEBRUARY 28. Clear. Went out prospecting and took a hole intending to work it next day. All well.

FRIDAY, MARCH 1. Commenced operation in the Oregon Canyan and laboured till evening, clearing the surface and intending to operate with our rockers on the next day, paying for the priviledge 3 oz. This day operations 12 of us took out 12$ We have no confidence in the location, but being the only location we can get do it as the best.

SATURDAY, MARCH 2. Snowed. Kept employed in keeping camp fires burning. Stormed all night.

SUNDAY, MARCH 3. Fine day spent in reading and laying in Camp. We are favoured with good health.

MONDAY, MARCH 4. Stormy, Snowing. Employed in making ourselves comfortable.

TUESDAY, MARCH 5. Worked our hole in the Canyon out. Made this day but 4$, making after hard labour in snow & mud & water 15$ for what we paid 3 oz. Have made up our minds to start a party prospecting on the next day.

WEDNESDAY, MARCH 6. Our contemplated plans all frustrated. Snow our doom. About 11 o'clock turned to rain, which fell in torrents, blowing a hurricane and storming all night. Our camp fires are quenched by the torrents of rain. Two of our party left camp for better and more comfortable accomodations.

THURSDAY, MARCH 7. Rained and snowed all day. Layed in camp.

FRIDAY, MARCH 8. A party of us consisting of 8 in number started out prospecting on the *Middle Fork*. Reached the River at 6 o'clock same day. Encamped after a tired march on the banks of the Middle Fork of the American at the foot of the Steepest Mountains I have ever seen, down which we had difficulty getting, as we were all over packed, having on our backs 50 lbs each.

SATURDAY, MARCH 9. In our explorations this day found the mouth of a beautiful creek up which we concluded to prospect. Returned to camp, ditermining to try our fortunes on this Creek which we have learned is called Otter Creek, on which we found no one at work and under the impression it never has been. We picked from between the Crevices of the Slate 25$ in scales, some of them weighing one dollar Each. We gathered this amount, 4 of us, in 3 hours.

SUNDAY, MARCH 10. Six of us started for the old camp in Oregon Canyon for implement, balance of party ditermining to encamp at Otter Creek, left at 8 o'clock in the morning and returned same evening heavily packed. We all rested poorly having over exerted ourselves.

MONDAY, MARCH 11. Moved our camp up Otter Creek having selected a beautiful spot. All around us is perfectly wild. We know of no white man near us.

TUESDAY, MARCH 12. Rained from Monday evening till 11 o'clock this day. Started out, and eight of us took out this day 4 oz, which we generally found in the crevices of the slate rock. The gold here is Coarse. Commenced raining at 5 o'clock.

WEDNESDAY, MARCH 13. Rained and hailed hard all night and all this day stayed in camp. Our camp fires are out.

THURSDAY, MARCH 14. Rain & hail.

FRIDAY, MARCH 15. Rain & hail. One of our party, G. Cochran from Ohio, he's sick. Four of our party left for our old encampment saying they would not be back till weather became settled, detirmining to remain there and consume their provisions before moving again.

SATURDAY, MARCH 16. This has been a clear and fine day. We flatter ourselves the weather has changed for the better. It is very acceptable as our Blanketts have become very wet and we have no opportunity of changing them. Six of us all that are left in camp save Cockran who is still in his Blanketts but seems better. We started out to work and laboured hard but with poor success having made 1½ oz this day. At the price of provisions here we are not making expenses, having paid 48$ for 50 pounds of Flour and 15 pounds of Pork. Our diet is almost solely Pork, Flour, Tea, & Coffee. Our flour is mostly made into Flap Jacks which with Flummox, when we have the ingredients, is great living. Flummox is made by mixing everything in camp up in one dish and Stewing it. This day Doct Wright, an Englishman, came over from an old Camp. Reported snow there one foot deep. It is an ill wind that blows no one good. Some traders were driving some cattle down the mountains today when one took a start and rolled over a steep precipiece till he was dead. Not having money to buy a quarter which they are packing to the river, we have laid our plans for what is left of the carcass.

SUNDAY, MARCH 17. This morning I started out to see what had been left of the unfortunate steer. I found a head and tail which I shouldered. The tongue had been taken out but we had a fine breakfast of Brains and are now preparing a pot of soup for dinner. Tomorrow we expect to dine on Ox tail Soup. We have neither salt nor pepper. We season with Pork. After breakfast I with the rest, partook of our Sunday feast, a clean shirt, good wash etc. and feel first rate. Would like to be at Meeting today with Lizzie, the Boys, and all my friends but such is life and can't be helped. We are busy today reading our Bibles, airing and drying our Bed Clothes, smoking our pipes, in general terms Luxuriating on Air.

MONDAY, MARCH 18. Started early and made about Three Dollars to the man. Corkan [Cochran] up and at work.

TUESDAY, MARCH 19. The [illegible] showers today made at 2$ to the man.

WEDNESDAY, MARCH 20. Laboured hard all day made about 4$ to the man. Gold is mostly corse and found near the surface but the labour is hard. We have to turn over large rocks.

THURSDAY, MARCH 21. Broke my watch crystal this day—we are from this day without time. Concluded this day to open a deep hole in the bank—worked hard all day. Made about 4$ to the man.

FRIDAY, MARCH 22. Continued digging in our hole but our prospects are all blasted, having struck the bare rock without Accomplishing Anything more—the gold all having been on the surface. Our hole is about 15 feet square and 5 deep, having removed rocks that the combined force of three could barely move with levers and all plans that our philosophy could bring to bear.

SATURDAY, MARCH 23. Having become disgusted disheartened, we sought another spot and made by hard labour about one dollar and 50¢ each by 10 o'clock, having started to move as usual by sun up, rising by daylight to prepair our breakfast. We average pretty much with the rest of our party. We are convinced that we are in a rich gold region but as it has never been explored we must needs meet with difficulty. An old miner I met a few days since on the river told me that the stream I was on must be rich but his objection to exploring it was that Grizzly Bare tracks were too thick. We have put a good deal of time in exploring but have not met the monster and as for myself I have no curiosity to see his honour the lords of the valley and mountains of this country.

Having laboured hard this day and our third partner, Cockran being unwell, my partner William High proposed we should work out thirty pans of dirt and appropriate the proceeds to buying molasses, which was readily agreed to by me. The amount we ran through in about an hour and 1/2 amounted to one dollar and ninety cents. We proceeded to the store some two or three miles distant with our bottle. Told the storekeeper to weigh our dust and give us the amount in mollasses. Not being enough to pay for a quart, he insisted that I should have it charged to me, price $2.50 per quart, which was done. Credit in the mines is Cheap. Store keepers trust anybody that asks it. On our way to the store we noticed a piece of gold about the size of a grain of wheat on the surface—stooped down and with our Knives got out in an hour 10$ lumps, anything from two to three dollars. Growing dark and bound to have our molasses, we gave up the hunt intending to make further exploration on Sunday morning, a day we try to keep sacred, but our curiosity is excited and we often think of home and make every turn to get there.

SUNDAY, MARCH 24. Being our day, High and myself, to cook. We rise before sun up. Got breakfast which always consists of Flap Jacks, Pork & Coffee or tea, and our other partner being sick we started to explore the discovery made the day before, with the understanding all we made was to belong to the two. We arrived at the Contemplated spot and with jack Knives and spoons and shovels panned out in four hours, 4 ounces of the glittering Metal, having infringed on the Holy Day till we were satisfied that the hole was worth working in. Retired to camp. Told our friends of our success—described the spot—they started out to examine into the merits of the case. I prepaired my meal Flap jacks, Coffee, & Pork, and the luxury Beans. Went down and plunged in the Creek—rubbed well with a rough towel—put on a change of clothing—read a few chapters in the Bible, smoked a segar and felt happy, fancied myself shortly bound for home. Our friends have returned and offered us 200$ for our claim. Told them I would not sell for twice that, nor would not give so much for such a plan till twas more fairly tested. Recommended them to take Claim near us, which they concluded to do. The deposits here are of such a singular character that I hardly dare flatter myself that we have struck the spot. The only thing is we will work it out and then try somewhere else. Two of our party left today for the old camp at Georgetown to bring over some provisions left there by us. We weighed our gold, the produce of this morning, and found it to be 4 oz. & 12 dollars—near 5 oz. Our party returned this evening heavily loaded and much exhausted.

MONDAY, MARCH 25. Commenced operations today in our new hole. In about one hour took out about 12 dollars, when it commenced raining, which lasted all day. With the commencement of rain ended our days operation so we lay in camp inactive.

TUESDAY, MARCH 26. Commenced operations, the weather being clear. Each of us being three in number, took out one ounce each.

WEDNESDAY, MARCH 27. Each one ounce.

THURSDAY, MARCH 28. Cockran sick and in his blankett. High and Myself took out thirty four dollars, charging Cochran four dollars each for our services and giving him an equal portion, making one ounce each for High and myself.

FRIDAY, MARCH 29. Cockran is still lain up, High and myself dug this day Thirty Two dollars divided amonst the three making each 10.65 each, adding Four dollars each to High and my proportion makes for the day Fourteen sixty five cents.

SATURDAY, MARCH 30. High and myself worked part of the day. Made Ten dollars having laboured Hard, concluded to devote the balance of the day to going to the store, washing ourselves and clothes so as to have Sunday as a day of rest. The stream we bathe in is such as you read of, the melted snows of the mountains and clear as a diamond and cold as ice, most delightfull for absolution and most palitable to the taste. Cockran is getting better. Our friends are all discouraged, having done but poorly this week. We are in good spirits about our hole. It seems to run well. There is no knowing when it may give out. May not last a week. My last [illegible] and if we can average as well as we are doing now we are doing as well as the best of Minors at this season, the waters being so high that they cannot get at the rich deposits which generally lay near and in the centre of the streams. We have selected a spot on Otter Creek which we intend damming when the waters fall. It is attended with a great deal of labour but if blessed with health all the rest is easy.

I sometimes wonder at the immense stone or rather rocks we succeed to move with our forlorn implements, depending generally on Main strength and stupidness which is a wonderfull Machine in the mines. Good diggings are mostly found where labour is the hardest.

I am at this time a more happy man that I have been since I landed in this country. The march of civilisation is onward. Some minors have encamped near us. We once reigned sole heirs to the creek. The Red man has even left our vicinity and his trail is being marked with the fresh grass and beautifull flowers which flourish where ever they can find space, to us an acceptable change giving us beauty [insert crossed out] for ferocity.

SUNDAY, MARCH 31. This has truly been a day of rest. The Bible has generally had its turn from each in camp. All is quiet and pleasant sounds as the day is fine. The regular, the only cloud around us as Paul used to say about his Hirdy Girdy and Flagolet that they was always regulars with him, so I say of pipes and Tobacco, they are our regulars here, the only luxury of Civilized life we indulge in that I am aware of.

MONDAY, APRIL 1. This day Cockran being able to work we all three turned to. Our days labour though arduous was not as profitable as sometimes. This day we took out but one ounce and one dollar in all.

TUESDAY, APRIL 2. This morning a proposition being made to commence operations for building a dam, High and myself concluded to operate with the ballance of our company, Cockran declining. He operates for himself at our old spot which we intend returning to as soon as the Dam and race are finished, which by the progress we have made to day will not take more than a week to know what our luck will be. I have no great faith in such operations. In many cases they have large sums of Gold taken by turning streams and in May it is labour lost.... Wrote Lizzie and Mother & Father, enclosed one ounce as specimen.

WEDNESDAY, APRIL 3. Having worked at our hole yesterday already and been moderately successful, and during the evening a proposition having been started to commence damming the creek, concluded to join in with the party in the operation. I have no great faith in its success, but thinking it best to move with the crowd and thinking how I should regret not having entered into it should my friends be successful, I think it best to be with them. Let the result be as it may. This day, two of our party having become discouraged, leave us in the morning. They say intending to go to the southern mines, Wm & Thos Williams. We regret to part with them. There are nine of us left. Succeeded in building part of our race this day.

THURSDAY, APRIL 4. Progressed quite rapidly with our race this day and succeeded in placing our timbers for the Dam. Our only tools are an axe and pickaxes and shovels.

FRIDAY, APRIL 5. This day it was concluded We should work our holes to make expenses for our Living. High, Cockran, Myself made this day about 28 dollars.

SATURDAY, APRIL 6. It rained hard all night previous and in the morning being extremely wet and disagreeable, pouring rain. Laid in our blanketts till eleven o'clock when it cleared off sufficiently to get breakfast. About 12 it cleared off. We all went to work in our holes and worked till about 4 o'clock. Our party made 10 dollars. We knocked off to go after provisions for the week—there are 4 in our mess. Our bill for the week we paid off, it was 29$—pork and Flour our food.

SUNDAY, APRIL 7. Unfortunately for us this is a wet and disagreeable day so we cannot air our blanketts, which is Very essential as it drys them. Our wardrobe being the tops of bushes, as a matter of course our clothing is all wet—we are denied the luxury of a change.

MONDAY, APRIL 8. Rain until about 4 o'clock this afternoon—the clouds breaking give every promise of a fair day tomorrow. We discovered a drove of Deer immediately over our tent and near the summit of the mountain. High started out with my rifle in pursuit. In about an hour and a half we noticed him rise from behind a peak just above his game. Next visible to our sight was smoke and almost simultaneously came rol[l]ing pell mell as we thought [a] mortally wounded deer. He was so satisfied that it was a death shot that he reloaded and succeeded in getting a second shot at the retreating herd. Not seeing one fall he took it for granted that he has missed his game. He returned to take charge of the first shot when, lo, he was not there. It growing dark, could not hunt for the lost deer—returned to camp and in the morning (Tuesday 9th) an expedition started out to find our game but returned about one o'clock unsuccessful. Worked from 2 tonight at mining with poor success.

WEDNESDAY, APRIL 10. High, Cockran and Myself made this day after hard labour about eight ounces each. Two of the camp started out to look for a pair of boots which one had lost on the mountain when to our surprise they returned with the Boots, and, most important to the camp, the Deer that had been shot by High two days before upon which we are now luxuriating.

THURSDAY, APRIL 11. Having just heard of some very rich Diggings which have just been discovered in a Canyon between the North & Middle Fork of the American and about 22 miles distant at what is called Birds store, the company in camp appointed a young man from Virginia by the name of Scott and another, Gilbert Hogan from New Orleans and myself to go over and secure a claim. We started about 1 o'clock, each packing a pair of blanketts and provision sufficient to last four days. We had some high mountains to cross. Were astonished to meet so many persons on their return, which induced us to enquire of the various partys we met. Their accounts all agreed with each others statements, which were to the effect that some person had taken large amounts out of the canyan last fall, that the waters were so high it could not be worked before the first of June. The number of people who had collected were from two to three thousand—all idle, waiting for the fall of the water, *Gambling* the sole occupation. There had been a few persons shot there a few days ago. Summing all up, considering it probable the society would be bad and success not certain, After reaching within about 10 miles of the point, we concluded to return to our camp on Otter Creek and report, which Move proved acceptable to our Camp.

I was much surprised on returning to camp, it being night, to see seated round our fire Fred, Ned Iddings and Ned Pierce.[11] They brought me of all things most prized a letter. It was from Lizzie and was encouraging, also one from Joseph Hobson of San Francisco giving me an account of 2400$ to collect in Vernon, he thinking I was still in Sacramento.[12]* This has given me some uneasiness, as I deposited some money in Sacramento for a Friend and knowing he would mention if he received a letter, I wrote, just before leaving, the fact to J. Hobson who has always been kind to me. My three friends had [been] driven from Sacramento, the "Amphibious," by two important causes—a Threatening Flood and a desire to breathe the mountain air, on which I assured them they can flourish and fatten.

FRIDAY, APRIL 12. We operated today digging—our success but poor, averaging abut 6$ each. Fred and his party, I advised to lay down and gain strength before operating.

*Hobson's letter and account follow JMS's diary.

SATURDAY, APRIL 13. We made from work to-day averaged about 5$ each. Had to scold Fred today about eating Flap Jacks and wound up by telling him I would rather see him take Arsenic in small doses than Flap Jacks when he was labouring under an attack of dysentary, but Fred knows best that I will always give him my advice.

SUNDAY, APRIL 14. Today spent as a day of rest as [illegible] always ready for the mines.

MONDAY, APRIL 15. All Hands at work on the Dam and race. Fred, Iddings & Pierce anxious to go to work. Busy exercising my oratory to persuade them to get fully recruited, not disposed to take advice. I mention here with rejoicing that two letters Fred lost of mine, I received on Sunday by offering and paying Ten Dollars. On opening the package there turned out three, which was great satisfaction—one from Father Tyson & two from Lizzie. Accounts from home all satisfactory.

TUESDAY, APRIL 16. Fred and part of days labour broken down. I was glad to see Fred as a Brother but when I think of his imprudence coming where there are no comforts—no nothing and so hemmed in with . . . [Diary ends here].

• • • • •

San Francisco, February 21 1850

To John Marsh Smith

We have written to Mssrs Booker & Brand herewith instructing them to pay you the *Ammt* of acct on presentation.

DEAR JOHN

Herewith I send you a letter from the house with an acct for collection in Vernon. The parties we know very little about but were introduced to us from a respectable quarter. We have heard nothing from them and therefore wish you to stir them up and if you find any certain mode of compelling them to pay make them do so. I doubt their integrity because they have let the time when the amt was due from nearly a month without any explanation to us.

I enclose a letter to you from home. When do you go to the diggings? The steamer not in from Panama but expected momentarily.

Yours truly
Joseph Hobson

•   •   •   •   •

San Francisco, February 21 1850

To John Marsh Smith
Sacramento City
Dear Sir

Enclosed we have you an Acct. against a firm in Vernon amounting to Twenty four hundred and Seventy dollars due agreeable to terms of sale 30th of last month.

If convenient we will thank you to go to Vernon and present the acct. for payment and use such means to recover the amount or to secure it as your judgment may point out, advising us of the result. We will allow you 5 pct. on amount recovered and your expenses.

Yours truly
Cross Hobson & Co.

•   •   •   •   •

San Francisco, February 21 1850

To Messrs Booker & Brand
Vernon

Presented by Mr. John M Smith
Messrs Booker & Brand
Vernon
Dear Sirs

We have sent herewith to Mr. John Marsh Smith of Sacramento for collection, an Acct. against you for purchase mdse [merchandise] of us on the 30th Nov. last the amount of Twenty four hundred & Seventy dollars.

The mdse was sold to you on a credit of two months, and the amount was therefore due on the 30th of January last. We deviated from an established rule when we gave you a credit, believing that you would pay promptly at maturity.

Should Mr. Smith present the account you will please pay him.

YOURS RESPECTFULLY
Cross Hobson & Co.

Messrs. Booker & Brand
Vernon

(2 mos credit) To Cross Hobson & Co San Francisco

1849
Nov 30   To 49 Bags Beans @$10 . . . . $ 370.00
    "   To 75 Bags Flour ea 175 lbs—65 5/8 Bags @ $32 . . . 2,100.00

2,470.00

Pay the above amount to Mr. John Marsh Smith, San Francisco February 21 1850.

Cross Hobson & Co.

•   •   •   •   •

Otter Creek, 6 days above Sacramento
April 7 1850

To Harriet S. Tyson

Your kind and very acceptable letter written in September last did not reach me until some time in February. Say to brother Jim, I have no occasion for a horse and buggy to hunt up a trout stream— within twenty feet of our tent flows Otter Creek, a mountain creek such as you *read of*, its water deep, clear as an emerald and rapid as the imagination can depict a stream flowing through a mountainous region, leaping from abyss to abyss at every bound and filled with Fish of the most delicate order. The mountains on this side of the stream are grand, almost perpendicular and towering to the skies, frequently of soil bare of heavy timber but rich in quantity and beauty of its flowers.

It is useless for me to say how my thoughts dwell upon home, Lizzie, our dear little boys and dear friends. The labor attending gold-digging is nothing when crowned with success. Our diet is hardly calculated for a laboror, but all I ask is health and I will work hard and give digging a fair test. I have not been particularly successful but feel encouraged to dig on, I would rather make my money by digging than by merchandising but expect to give the latter a trial about July next, and as soon as I make my pile I will be with you. I want you to cheer Lizzie up as much as you can. She must feel no uneasiness about me, and as for Fred he has grown to be a perfect worker. He is very hardy and strong and I think will make money, he is quite a *financier*. He sent me word he intended to go teaming, he owned when I left Sacramento a pair of mules and waggon worth six hundred dollars.

SUNDAY, APRIL 14. This is one day of rest, and having the time I take advantage of it to continue this epistle. The past week has been attended with such favorable results as my heart desires but "hope on hope ever," such is life. We have had some rainy days during the week. We spent one day in hunting which resulted in killing a deer, upon which we are now feasting. Today we have a roaring pot of soup on, I have just put in the seasoning, mustard, nutmeg, salt and pickles so as to make it *vegitable*. We could get a deer very frequently, as we often see them feeding on the mountains that overhang our camp, but cannot spare the time, so confine ourselves to hog and flour generally, flapjacks and pork today for breakfast dinner and supper and tomorrow pork and flapjacks for breakfast dinner and supper and that is not all. It goes first rate always.

On Thursday last I started with three others for some rich diggings, known to but few, distant about 22 miles and over mountains that truly made me feel our own insignificances. In these mountains a man in reality becomes half horse or half mule, for no one thinks of an expedition without packing himself with blankets and provisions and so becomes a *beast* of burden. Of the former we each started with one pair, and of the latter, enough for four days. We had proceeded but part of a day when we struck a fresh trail and were astonished to find it so well defined, but when the wind blew you might *almost* by the cloud of dust raised and the first reflection satisfied me that the silent rumor was a perfect tell-tale and though it whispers, how fast travels the news of the new Eldorado as I understand tis called. The news of it had been sounded aloud some two weeks e'er we heard it in our solitude, and immense numbers were now seen crowding on in hot haste to lay claim to their 20 ft.

We met numbers on their return to old haunts with a quisical smile on their countenances which I readily translated into "humbug" and we concluded to make inquiry. All told the same story, that some promising indications had manifested themselves by the success of the labors of a few, some one or two had struck good leads and taken out large amounts. The common would, if deeded off from one end to the other, give 20ft each to a thousand men, and that already between two and three times that number were now quartered at the point, waiting the falling of the waters which will not be low enough to work before June so with a prospect of two months idleness and after that a fight for a claim we were satisfied 'twas better to make back tracks, which opinion being unanimous before eight o'clock the same evening we reached our camp on Otter Creek, where our return was hailed and our report proved satisfactory.

I was utterly astonished on looking around to find in camp Fred, Ned Iddings, and Ned Peirce. They brought me a letter from Lizzie dated in October which was very satisfactory and pleasant. The above mentioned gentlemen vamoused from Sacramento to escape the flood, which now promises evil to that amphibious city, and to lead their lungs to better pasture and exchange the putrid smell of a stock of filth for the pure air and crystal ice cold water such as we are blessed with on this ranch. They have come to rusticate.

I sent written instructions to Fred by no means to send my letters from home into the mountains to me, but unfortunately he having met with a good opportunity sent three, which he believes one was from Lizzie, another he thinks from my brother, and the other he knows not whom. I gave him a blowing up about it and told him the next time he did so I would give him a dose of *Castor oil*. There ain't no use of crying about spilt milk. The author that referred to them wise words must have meant the milk of cows and untamed asses, but letters is the milk of Human Kindness and the loss of them is worth weeping for in this vast wilderness by us who repose in solitary grandeur under tall cedars on the mountain tops or in the valleys, who burrow in the ground and cradle all day and pan out at eve their spoils, returns to camp with appetite keen as the winter winds, *spreads* our repast on a portion of this universe, for the native earth is our table and the seat of our well-worn breeches the only arm chair we set in. When them goes we lays back in our shirt tails and holds on by our teeth, after devouring our prey which we generally does whole, it being mostly spoon victuals. We smokes and retires smoking and very shortly retires in the arms of an omnibus.

YOUR BROTHER AFFECTIONATELY,

J. Marsh Smith

At Georgetown, April 23 1850

Postscript

Fred's trip to the mountains I am sorry to say been of no advantage to him. I am now at this place for a doctor. I left camp yesterday. I considered Fred better, he suffers from great debility, the mountains by which we are walled in are so steep that a mule cannot pack a man off. As soon as I can get him well enough I shall take him to San Francisco and insist on his going home as soon as I can find some friend or companion for him. My time and money shall be devoted to his comfort. He is not confined to his bed but requires a good deal of waiting on. Remember, to dear Lizzie and all. I am well, would write Lizzie but have not time. I brought this epistle over with me, not expecting a chance of sending it. If Freds sickness continues my plans for the summer will be knocked into pie but such is life. Our dam and race are nearly completed. I have not been compelled to lay up for one day with sickness since I have been in the mountains and trust to God I may be favored. I enclose a specimen.

Remember me to Jim. I will by first opportunity to Lizzie

[On outside of letter] Don't drop the small package of Gold inside

• • • • •

To Elizabeth Brooke Smith
DEAR LIZZIE

Two of our camp becoming discouraged, one Dr. Wright an Englishman and a very pleasant Gentleman and one of the Proprietors of a Hospital in Sacramento, the other Equally agreeable by the name of Hogan from New Orleans, I part with them with regret. They leave to morrow Monday for Sacramento-the-Amphibious, tired of their poor success and hard work. They leave just as the mining season commences.

I cannot brag on my great success this far but this much I can say, that High and myself have done better than any other two of our camp and better than any that we have heard of in our receipts. Tis true there are but few here but we have had a good deal to contend with. Cockran who we took in with us as a partner has not been able to do a full days work since he has been in the mines and has had an equal share of the proceeds of our labour, and has now left us, sick, bound for the Hospital at Georgetown. Our partnership is dissolved. High and myself now. Cockran left some debts unpaid which High and myself have to pay for him.

I have had a good deal to discourage me since I arrived in this Country *but hope on hope ever is my motto*, and still feel as if success must be mine. I was in hopes ere this I would have been enabled to remit my kind Brothers and Friends the amount they so generously loaned me. Tell them all that if the Health which I am now so favoured with continues it will be forth coming.

I wrote Harriett, and on Tuesday last at Fred's request after a hard days labour from sun up till 3'oclock left Georgetown to bring over a Dr. Cauly, an acquaintance of Fred's and also of mine. Tis true we had a good Dr. in camp whose services were liberally offered me gratis, but Fred don't like anything thats cheap. So I to gratify him done as he ordered, he don't often request. Thee knows well he orders when he is sick.

I am astonished at myself to find how I have improved in climbing mountains. It was four o'clock before I commenced to ascend the mountain that over hangs our camp. I sat down to rest but once and made the summit in one hour and before night was eating a good supper in Georgetown, intending to leave the same night for camp, but when I became over heated I found I was a little tired so concluded to wait til morning. I slept with Dr. Cauly in his hospital, representing Freds case. Left early in the morning for camp, the Doctor promising to come over after dinner or as soon as he could procure a *mule*. I always travel on foot. I took it more leisurely, found I could make but half day, and got into camp at 12 o'clock and was away for work and succeeded in making half day on the dam. The Doctor visited Fred and prescribed. Gave him pills to take, some kind of Solution and Dover's powders to give should the Medicine have too forceful an effect,[13] and mixed some Tartar and Grease to rub on his breast to make it sore, which effect it has had and Fred is now certainly better and gaining in strength. I do not like the Doctor ordering him brandy to drink.[14] He has promised me that if he can procure any good wine in Georgetown to send me over some to administer instead. I can say Lizzie ours is truly a temperate camp, the only ardent spirits that has ever been in it I have purchased by the advice of the Doctor solely for Fred. I pay four dollars per bottle for it.

I must confess Fred is not strong enough for this country. Last fall when he was ill I tried to get him in the notion of going home but without avail, but now it is pretty well understood that the first Six Hundred dollars made by either of us goes to paying his expenses to that end, as my expenses are so greatly increased by Freds sickness. I have made up my mind to relinquish my interest in the dam for the present and strike as I have been advised into some of the Caniens [canyons] about 20 miles higher up on Otter Creek. My advisor represents them as very rich and but little worked. My partner High goes with me and I think Ned Pearce will accompany us. We pack on our backs implements, a pair of blankets each and as much provision as we can carry. There are plenty of deer in the mountains and an abundance of fish in the stream.

I must tell Thee a compliment Dr. Cauly paid me when we came into Camp. It was his remark that I was the most healthy looking man in the camp. I try to take good care of myself, finding Grease and flap Jacks not to agree with me sometimes. Since I altered my mode of Grit and now live on Dry ship bread—tea—and mush I do not think I eat as much Fat in a week as anyone here in camp does for one day. I am just about the colour of a piece of Sole Leather.

When at Georgetown I sent enclosed a trifling amount of Gold of my own digging to thee and Harriet and addressed thee a post script. Ned Iddings has promised to pay every attention to Fred during my absence as it is impossible to get him out of the mountains till he gets stronger as they are too steep to pack up. Shanks mare is the only horse a man can ride up hill here. I want thee to write me by every mail. I always write to thee when an opportunity affords. It will be a great treat to get a big pile of letters from home when I go down. I have sent instructions down by no means to send my letters into the mountains, as they are most always sure to be lost. I sent the same Word to Fred but he did not heed it and sent in an envelope by some good opportunity, and for a long time they were lost and never would have heard of them had not Fred come up. A reward of 10$ brought them in a few days, their dates Christmas night, January 9 from Father Jan 10 1850 from Thee and a pleasant letter, all truly acceptable.

Dear Lizzie I want to write a dozen letters. Sunday is our only day of rest and tis now 12 o'clock and this is all I have accomplished, how shall I get through. I must enclose thee a few little specimens of my labour. I enclose thee an ounce some time since, which ere this thee will have received, Love to all and say to them at home they must excuse my neglect in writing them. When one swings pick or shovel all day he is apt to seek for rest on his back when every opportunity affords. I never have received a copy of the *Tribune* since I have been in the Country. If letters and papers are not directed to care of Cross Hobson & Co. I never get them.

FROM THY AFFECTIONATE

J. Marsh Smith

[On outside of letter] I intended enclosing some specimens but only meeting with an opportunity to Sacramento think it best not to risk it as the letter may be lost.

JMS

[The following was enclosed.]

Otter Creek, 6 days above Sacramento
Sunday, April 28 1850

To Gilbert Tyson Smith and
Thomas Marsh Smith
DEAR LITTLE GILLIE & TOMMY

This letter Father writes to you he want you to be good boys. You must love one another and be kind to all the little Boys you play with and when those that love you, particularly your good Mother and Grand Mothers and Grand Fathers, Uncles and Auntys, tell you when you are naughty you must tell them you are sorry and will try and be good Boys. You must not pull Grand Mother's Flowers without consent and dont eat any Green Fruit in the summer. Uncle Fred sends his love to you.

FROM
Father

• • • • •

Otter Creek near Fords Bar
Middle Fork, May 14 1850

To Elizabeth Brooke Smith
DEAR LIZZIE

I have taken advantage of every opportunity that has afforded since I left Sacramento to write thee. After the labour of weeks we have succeeded in turning the water sufficiently to work in the bed of the stream. Engaged in this employment have we all been for the last two days like *mud turtles* floundering in the mud in slush, and after striking several well formed pockets which we worked out without any success, has satisfied us that the deposits here will not pay, for the gold in the bottom of the creek being mostly very fine, and that on the surface coarser, satisfies me the coarse deposit is of recent date and wont pay. I want to get where it has been accumulating for ages. On the strength of our disappointment, Ned Pierce left this morning for Sacramento without any intention of ever testing the mines again. My partners High and Ned Iddings leave this afternoon for the same destination with no intention of returning, and by them I forward these lines.

Fred is fast gaining strength, and so soon as he gets able to ascend the mountain that he shall do so and take up his quarters at George Town with Doct. Cauly, a Gentleman who came out with us and who attended him while sick in camp. Fred thinks it hard I should sometimes scold him for eating too much.

It is my intention now I am pretty much deserted by my old companions to remove and take up my quarters on the Middle Fork, and satisfy myself with making expenses till the waters fall. I am sure I have given Otter Creek a fair trial, and am encouraged to content myself with small gains on the river till the snows melt and the waters fall. I would much rather make my money mining than by any other process and the society of the mines is probably better than that of the cities. The people of the mines are generally temperate and we are no loss for society of the most refined Gentleman. From what I can gather, the health of the Country or part rather I am now in is considered good. I have enjoyed most excellent health since I have been here and have laboured every day save two and the acceptable Sundays, weather permitting. The highest I have known the thermometer here was 92. I have suffered none from heat, and sleep soundly at night.

Dear Lizzie, give thyself no uneasiness about me. I care about no comforts here while blessed as I am with health, trusting the day is not far distant when I may be permitted to return to Thee, our little ones and friends, in the character of a lucky miner. I assure Thee, Dear Lizzie I will be satisfied with this beat and when I get home I dont want to leave it no more. I think I would be satisfied just to play about in the yard with the boys. Tell my kind creditors that I think of them often when I sling my *pick and shovel*. I am on desire, nothing preventing, to give mining a fair test this season and if I meet with no success then I will try something else. Love to all.

THINE AFFECTIONATELY
J. Marsh Smith

(Fred has promised me to write home)

(I hear no news therefore I can communicate none)

Dear Gillie

Thee must try to learn and write me a letter. Be good to little brother Tommy and mind what dear Mother tells thee.

Father

• • • • •

Sacramento City, May 30 1850

To Elizabeth Brooke Smith
DEAR LIZZIE

I arrived in this city day before yesterday with Fred, anticipating starting him home in the first steamer then returning myself to the mines. Fred feels so much better that all the persuasion and argument I can use to get him home is of no avail. I consider his case requires such comforts and care as are not to be found in this country.

I write now in haste, will by next steamer write thee a letter. I rec'd quite a lot of letters on my arrival here for Fred and myself, about *Twenty*. Have rec'd from Smith & Atkinson Two Invoices and Bills of Lading Ref Goods Shipped per *Catherine*.[15] She has not yet arrived. Also accounts of shipments made by Tony. Kind letters from Thomas M. and Father Tyson. The steamer leaves in a few minutes. I have not time to say much. I am enjoying first rate health. Love to all, will give the business entrusted to my charge my best care and attention. Feel much obliged. If I feel justifiable by any good opportunity that may offer for trade I may take advantage of Thy Father and my Brother Thomas offer. I will write them all, Father, brother Thomas, Robert, Tony by next steamer. Love to all,

FROM THY AFFECTIONATE

J. Marsh Smith

I met George Evans in this [place][16]

•　•　•　•　•

Baltimore, April 30 1850

To John Marsh Smith or Frederick Tyson
Care of Cross Hobson & Co
San Francisco
DEAR JOHN

I wrote to you in February enclosing BLI & Invoice of Adamantine & Tallow candles on board ship *Catherine* & Schooner *Laura Bevan.* If you have received them and have not sold them, and there appears to be a tendency downward please close them out if you can get enough to pay invoice price and expenses, as the quantity going forward may cause the price to go very low. However use your own discretion in the matter. They are an article that are always wanted and the large population of California will require a great many. It is estimated that 100,000 people will have left the west for California this year.

George Hobson and three of his daughters are here, William & wife have been here intended going on to Philadelphia today. I heard John Wethered was to start for California today, William Norris going on the 15th of this month. Lizzie will write by him, all well at home. James Atkinson has been quite unwell but is better. He looks badly, has had a very bad cough. All well at Nathan Tysons. Bill Handy started for California about six or seven months ago. They have not heard of his arrival yet, went in the ship *Silas Baldwin* from Philadelphia. Gill was at our house to dinner today, went after dinner with Father to get a top, I sent you a newspaper last week and will also send one today. Richard Brown has got home. He told me he saw you in California. Thomas wrote to Cross Hobson & Co on 13th March with Invoices and Bills Lading of my candles enclosed, as it seemed doubtful whether you would get those forwarded to you.

YOURS AFFECTIONATELY
AM Smith

The candles on the Ship *Catherine* are Tallow, those on the *Laura Bevan*, adamantine Branded Belmont Sperm. I will direct this to you or Fred as you may be out of the way of getting it for some time.

DEAR FRED

If John has appointed any one to take charge of my lots candles please call on the party or parties and tell them not to hold on to them if they can get enough to bring me out square, as the quantity of Candles gone to California may cause the price to go low. All well at your home. Ned Ferris through town the other day on his way west on business.

Fred write to me; have you seen anything of John Shore. I gave him a letter of introduction to you. Bill George has been taking Polka lessons, you ought to see him dancing around Bacon Hogshead. Bob Tyson will perhaps take lessons next winter, what a perfect swell he will be. Samuel Steel is home, has been very sick since he got home. Fred, when you and John are ready to come home do come when the Isthmus is healthy. One of George Hobsons daughters took the Chagres fever though I suppose had it slightly. If my shipment dont turn out good I will have to stop the shipping business. Good bye.

YOURS
AM Smith

Bob has just come into the counting room, says he has not received that box of gold yet.

· · · · ·

To John Marsh Smith
DEAR SIR

This will be handed you by my friend Mr. Charles Moore who visits the land of Ophir on business. Any attention and information that you can afford him will be esteemed a personal favor to myself, and I know that you will take pleasure in assisting him to the extent of your ability for the sake of your old friend.

John Curlett, Jr.

Mr. Moore has had the great kindness to take charge of a package for you from my wife*

· · · · ·

Sacramento City, June 14 1850

To Elizabeth Brooke Smith
DEAR LIZZIE

I wrote thy Father and Tony some three or four days since. In the letter to Father I gave particular reference to Freds *Sailing.* I have had nothing from the Bay and take it for granted Fred is now making good way toward home. He surely would soon have been taken sick if he had detirmined to remain here. The climate does not suit him by any means.

I have been enjoying most excellent health, but am now unfortunately a sufferer to some extent. The Doctor says I am suffering from poison so common in this country that it may be considered one of the prevailing diseases here. It is confined to my body and affects my sistem something as a tooth ache does and renders me too uneasy to write.

I fancy I can see light ahead and am only waiting to get well to take advantage of it. I do not wish to say any more on this till I find I

---

*The contents are mentioned in JMS's postscript to Lizzie, June 14 1850.

am not to be disappointed. I have had the only good offer made me since my return here from San Francisco that has been suggested to me by any one in this country, and as soon as I feel able will most certainly drive ahead.

Business is extremely dull here, verry little trading going on—it is expected business will commence about Middle of July and the prospect is that by that time I will have a store in operation. It is not expected that so much will be made by the merchants this fall as was last. Goods are on the decline. The retailer does not make the enormous profit of last year. I have taken advantage of Fathers Kindness and drawn on him for *500*$. It was a *sore lick*. Have been induced to believe from a friend of mine here that I will have no further necessity of drawing on Home for ballance offered by Thos & Father.

I have the most comfortable home here that tis been my lot to luxuriate in for months. I am now encamped at the House of a friend of mine from Baltimore named R. Merrill of the firm of Rose-Merrill & [Dodge or Lodge] of Baltimore but now a partner of an old Californian by the name of Hensly—*Bankers*. It is at *Merrills* suggestion that I am induced to remain in Sacramento City. He is a very clever fellow, a friend of *Charly Kemps*.

It is very well that I left the Mines to bring Fred down, there are accounts just recd of tremendous rich deposits on the shore of a lake just discovered and about 100 miles from here where they wash from 1 oz to 300$ to a pan. They say on Deer Creek persons have left claims for which they paid 5000$ and gone to the lake. I must confess that I believe but little of it. Some shrewd trader is at the bottom of it I expect.

I recd from Thee Thine of Feb 3rd, Feb 24th, March 12, March 25th & Apl 10th. Also numerous and very acceptable from Robt, Thomas, Father Tyson, J. Curlitt, & Tony. I am and must if I can answer all, but if thy only could imagine how a fellow felt that was suffering from the poison of the country thy would hardly expect any letter from me this time.

I have the can[dles]. Say to Robt & Tony put the Invoices & Bills of Lading for *Catherine* and *L. Bevans* in to the Hands of Cross Hobson & Co. provided I should not be in San Francisco, they to take charge of them. The vessels have neither of them arrived yet. Candles do not appear brisk though prices keep up say 60¢ on Shore. Say I will give them my attention. Dear Lizzie, give my love to Mother & Girls, Boys, little ones, to all.

To Gillie & Tommy

I recd the letter you wrote little Boys. Am glad to hear you are first rate boys. Be good and dont give dear Mother more trouble than you can help.

Father

Dear Lizzie I expect I will come out Jay Bird, yet no knowing. Say to Missus Curlett I recvd her kind present of a cap, the most magnificant affair in California. Give her My Respects, remember me to W.A. Talbott.

Thine

I cannot write any more today, my breast & back sting like a swarm of *bees* was on it. Such is life in California. When I get home I dont want to go away no more.

. . . . .

Sacramento City, June 27 1850

To Thomas Marsh Smith
Dear Thomas M

Your kind favour of Mch 26th was handed me by Joseph Hobson. The particulars of my visit to San Francisco I have made Elizabeth and Father Tyson familiar with, and as Fred has left for home trust ere this arrives he will have reached home. I have not written to you, it was not for want of inclination on my part you must be well aware, but mortified at myself by being unable to make favourable reports on my progress. It has not been owing to neglect or indolence on my part.

My hotel was a humbug. It never was fitted up and the Floods made a clean sweep of it. I lost nothing individually by the operation but made nothing. I determined then to strike for the mines. The snow acted as a barrier to me but their melting cornered me during most of the time. I had determined to give the mines a fair shake and do not think I should of left them for some months had it not been requisite for Fred's security. I prefer the mines and mountains of California to its *Sodoms* and *Gomorrahs.*

The kind offer you made me I shall not avail myself of at present. I drew on Father Tyson for Five Hundred dollars, the balance of his order I hold on reserve and will not use it unless I think I can make a sure thing of it. I have had the effect what little means I may want made me by a friend in this place. It was my desire to embark in some retail business, but not being able to secure what I considered a desirable location for such a business, have been compelled to embark in something more extensive.

Have taken a fine warehouse on I St[reet] near the river, and have nearly disposed of one entire cargo from N. York and have the promise of more. If you hear of any cargoes shipped direct for Sacramento from Baltimore, please mention me to the shippers. Hayden and Cole I understand cleared a vessel for this port. Our firm is Smith & Suydam, J. Marsh Smith and James Suydam. My partner is a son of Lambert Suydam of New York and seems to have many friends disposed to throw business in his way.[17] It is our present intention to connect the auction with our commission business.[18] I think Sacramento is destined to become a great place, probably take the lead of San Francisco.

I can advise no shipments to California. It is impossible to say to day what to morrow will bring forth in a California markett. There is no regular system by which the mercantile community here are regulated. They appear more the creations of impulse than of sound sensible reflection. All here is speculation of the wildest character, as for example it is no unusual thing here to sell goods what is called blind, the auctioneer professing not to know what is in the packages. A great many goods sold for freight & storage is sold in this way.

I have left Bills of Lading & Invoice of your shipment in hands of Cross Hobson with orders to sell on board if it can be done to any kind of an advantage, as expenses here are so exceedingly great.[19] Candles such as I believe yours to be are worth in this place 60¢, can hardly be called brisk. Articles that were a drug this time last year are now becoming scarce. Soap is advancing, good brown, 8¢ Coffee is also high, Green being worth 60¢. Last year there was at this time no sale, the market was glutted, Mining implements such as shovel & picks etc. are now in demand. Cheese and Butter are articles that have always maintained a good price. Lard has always paid, is worth now 20¢ packed in kegs. Dried fruit apples & peaches are selling now for 30 & 35¢ per lb. Salt Beef has always been a drug in this markett, is not worth first cost. The vessels have none of them arrived by which the candles have been shipped. I will write Robt.

I am still suffering a good deal of pain from the bite of some poisonous insect. The sore is on my breast. I wish to write John Curlett. Return my thanks to Missus Curlett for her kind present. I rec'd Mothers kind favour on Feb 8th forwarded from Panama Mch 24th by Geo. Fisher. This letter I got out of the offices 22nd day of June. This is my last from Mother. Mother makes some enquiry of a Joseph Cross in this country. I learn there is such a man but have not come across anyone that knew him. I will write you again. Say to Toney do not come to this country. I shall leave it as soon as I get my pile.

YOUR BROTHER
J. Marsh Smith

My best regards to Mrs. Curlett & John. Remember me to Missus Talbott. I trust the day may come shortly when I can remit the favours of my friends.

JMS

· · · · ·

To Elizabeth Brooke Smith
DEAR LIZZIE

I have been anxiously looking for letters since the arrival of the mail—an acquaintance of mine from this place called at Cross Hobson & Co but brought me nothing.

I am satisfied there is something for me somewhere and think John Wethered must have something for me.

I have been nearly Twelve months buffitting with the crosses of this country, and hope now I am fixed—My general health is good, and trust I may be favoured. Comforts in California are things I hardly look for and seldom think of, and in fact care not for them here—I leave them for those bright latter days I anticipate my return amongst you. There is but one thing binds me to this hateful country, that is *gain.* All I want is my pile, when I leave the ranch with all dispatch. Iniquity reigns here in its most malignant forms, its greatest sufferers are I think the children of Citizens—here it is really terrific. I have seen little fellows here gambling in the streets, hardly high enough to look upon the top of a half Barrel, putting their five and ten cent pieces down on a card with as much coolness as the oldest vetran in the vice would stake his ounce. If I had to live in California, I would desert its populous places and take to its mountains.

I have no fault to find with the manner in which I am treated. All are kind to me and my immediate associates are Gentlemen in all respects, therefore I have a chance of passing most of my time pleasantly. My partner here in business I have but one fault with, I fear he is too much like myself. It is no use to explain thee knows me. I have tried to be *mean once* or *twice,* but it aint no use so I give it up. My partner's name is James Suydam, son of Lambert Suydam of N. York—President of the Union Insurance Co. of N.Y. A little while ago, I was a digger, my uniform a pair of Pantaloons, red shirt and cocked hat, with face and head overgrown with hair, and a skin the colour of burnt coffee, lived on pork and hard bread. Now and only of late, I appear as a dignified merchant, wear a clean shirt, eat at the best Hotels, talk as big as any one of Shipments from the States, of our increasing trade with China, and the ultimate result from the spread of the Angle Saxon race along the shores of the Pacific and when I am able to remit money home kind friends favoured me with, I will then feel like some Punkins.

I am very much in hopes Toneys & Roberts shipments may turn out favourable. They would pay if here now. I am daily looking for the arrival of the Vessel with them, having placed them in the hands of Cross Hobson & Co., provided I am not in San Fransisco to take charge. James Lea is doing well and appears a great favourite with the Missourians—he was very kind to Fred when sick. Ned Pearce is at work here—I see Ned frequently.

Kiss the dear little boys for me and tell them I send my love for them to be good Boys—Missus Curlett sent me most an elegantly worked Cap, for which thee must give her my thanks.

I have taken advantage of Father's offer, to the extent of 500$— having drawn on him for that amount. I will not draw for the balance nor on TMS without I see a chance of making a wise thing of it—I can get what I want for business purposes here at present.

Love to Bell, Anne, Lucy and all[20]—remember me to Harriete and tell me if she recd my letter from the *Mines*. I hope ere this reaches Fred will be with you.

Thine

J. Marsh Smith

Say to Mother Smith I will write her soon—I am a miserable scribe.

[The following was enclosed.]

Sacramento City, June 29 1850

To Elizabeth Brooke Smith
Dear Lizzie

I write thee without opening to thy last dates read by me, I have rec'd nothing as yet of the last mail, am satisfied that there are letters for me some where in the country, and think John Wethered must have something for me. I am just getting better from a severe sore on my breast—doct thinks was poisoned from the bite of some poisonous varmant. The steamer's Bell rings and I am selling some goods. If I get chance will write more. Love to all dear Lizzie. Kiss the little Boys. Adieu.

THINE

J. Marsh Smith

Will try and write by the Sacramento mail.

•   •   •   •   •

[postmarked] *Baltimore, Md.*

Thirt [*sic*] day [1850]

To John Marsh Smith

DEAR JOHN

I have not received a letter from you since your departure for California. I wrote you about [illegible] some time since with Invoice of Candles pr *Laura Bevan* & Ship *Catharine*, which letter I suppose you did not get on its arrival in California, you having gone to the mines, but no doubt you will get it on your return. The article appears to have declined in price but there must be a great demand for them from the immense numbers of people having gone to California and they being an article that are always wanted, though on account of the great quantity of Candles gone they may be low for some time. Write me and let me know something about the article. I put mine up in small packages, I hardly expect to retire on the proceeds of this shipment but will do very well from the present prospects if I get a very small profit. I gave your instructions in reference to the proceeds of the sales of my Candles in my letter with the invoices. If they sell at a profit, remit me anuff [enough] to pay for them and if you can use the balance of the money on your own account you can keep it for the present, but let me know what they sell for and the expences of them in Cal.

Thomas sent duplicate Invoices & Bills Lading of my Candles to Cross Hobson & Co that they might attend to them if you were not in S. Francisco to do so, receipt of which letter C H & Co. have acknowledged, but I wish you to do with them as you think best if you are in San F.

Thomas wrote to you about three months ago to draw on him for one thousand dollars and I think he also said if you saw a prospect of going into business you might draw on him for a thousand dollars more, the latter thousand as a loan which with the shipment of Candles will give you a start. You must have had a hard time in Cal.

Harriet received a letter from you some days since in which you mention Fred's indisposition. I suppose the family will look out for him in every steamer from Charges.

David Ives has gone and goes very soon to Central America to take charge of the Nicaragua road and they expect to have it in operation very soon.[21] When you are ready to come home perhaps it would be the best way for you to come.

George Hobson intends starting for the white sulpher springs tomorrow.[22] I think his daughters are going with him. I do not know whether William and his wife are going. William has brought a house near the monument back of where Howards had use to live.

Mary and Ellen are at Summer Hill.[25] Sallie is going down this week. The Oil speculation did not turn out as we were led to expect as it went down in price too soon for us but we have had a good year, made say 6 or 7000$ and sold a little over 94,000 Galls year ending tomorrow which will be the 1st.

I think Lizzie has written by this mail.

I know Annie Tyson has. Lizzie intends staying at Betsey Lees where she is at present.

Ned Cobb is home, has quite recovered, Landstreet is also.

Robert M. sends his love to you, says he hopes to hear of your being established in some regular business.

I heard of that speech at Sacramento. You somewhat alarmed the Hon Senator from California when you told the people you were a Whig, William Talbot says he intends being introduced to him when he goes to Washington and ask him about it.[24]

The Hon gentleman said they had a very enthusiastic meeting at Sac[ramento]. A man who said his name was Smith addressed the meeting but there was one thing he did not like about him, he said he was a Whig.

This is up to the latest moment, the mail closes directly. We are all well.

FROM THY AFFECTIONATE BROTHER
AM Smith

My love to Fred. Let me know what would likely be a good shipment. I have sent you newspapers several times.

• • • • •

Sacramento City, July 10 1850

To Elizabeth Brooke Smith
Matthew Smith
Sharp Street
Baltimore, Ma.
DEAR LIZZIE

As tis near the time for the departure of another steamer I will get in readiness a few lines for thee. When I last wrote which was but two weeks since my last mail—I was suffering from the bite of a musquito or some poisinous *varmant*. I am happy to say by this mail that I am relieved from severe suffering and trust I may not have an attack from any more such "Bipeds." The weather here is not warm, but hot, and I think will feel better than I did before I had the gathering on my Breast. A person here can be well and not feel first rate (the climate, thee can judge, must be peculiar). I try to be careful with my health by paying attention to my diet and do not expose myself to the sun or night air more than possible. There is a peculiarity about the atmosphere here that has never been noticed by the *scientific*, or if it has I have never heard of it. I have been told by old settlers here that if you hang beef say twelve or fifteen feet above the ground, it will keep good for many days, which if hung near the ground it spoils very soon, causing me to believe that there must be different and more pure atmosphere above than near the surface, and since I learned this fact I have taken to sleeping upstairs, and do not intend sleeping on the first floor if I can avoid it. In this country people cannot always do what they want.

Dear Lizzie, two steamers have arrived with mails and I have not yet had any letters save one by the last mail from Tony. Say to Tony when he writes to give me all the items. Sally and Ellen must help fill up. I heard they had written me but I have never yet seen the first outside shadow of a line from them. Tell Harriet to write and when she does to get some extract from brother Jim's log. I wrote her from the diggings and told her how we sat thare in our arm chairs and how we were sung to sleep by the song of the mountain torrent and all that kind of thing you call sentiment.

In my last I told thee I had embarked in business here and hope I may have as good luck as some others. Business here is dull at present, but every prospect of a speedy change for the better as there is a new trade opening and one that California never knew. A great many expeditions [are] preparing to fit out to carry provisions across the Sierra Nevada for the overland emigrants, some of who have already arrived, having left Independence as late as the 29th of April last. Say to Tony that the candles have not yet arrived. The mails are so uncertain between Sacramento and San Francisco that it is best to send my letters as usual to Cross Hobson & Co.

Kiss the dear little boys for me and tell them I want them to be good boys and mind what is said to them. My love to all. I trust ere this Fred is with you. He can give you an account of California, the heights of mountains on the forks of the American, and the depth of mud puddles in San Fransisco. James Lea told me to night at supper that he must write home and then gave as an excuse the sorry one that I have so often offered you. The careless manner in which mine were generally penned, that he had no place where he could sit down and write without continual interruption. Such is California. There is no place where one can retire. Jim is doing well and has a great many friends.

FROM THYNE AFFECTIONATELY
J. Marsh Smth

[On the same page]

Sacramento City, July 10 1850

To Catherine Marsh Smith

DEAR MOTHER

I wrote thee a few lines by steamer of the first. I have made enquirys trying to find out who Joe Cross is but have not learned. The first time I am in San Francisco I will ask Mr. Hopper of Cross Hobson & Co. as he has been for years a resident of the Sandwich Islands and would know Cross if he ever lived there. Say to Thomas M. that

> Things are as they is and
> cant be any Iser
> It tis as it tis and
> can't be any tiser
> (Such is life)

John Wethered has gone to the diggings and talks sanguine about taking out his pile. I wish him luck. While here he staid with me, was in good spirits and well. I look for him back daily, satisfied at seeing the elephant. This Sacramento is destined, I think, to be the great city of California. During the winter it suffered from a terrific flood that destroyed the prospects of many. The town was diminutive, buildings ordinary. The marks of the flood is still visible but none appear to heed it as a warning for the future, for larger and substantial buildings are taking the place of the camp House that was. I learn from a person who I met yesterday, and I have heard it rumoured before that good diggings have been discovered on the East side of the Sierra Nevada. There are large quantitys of provisions such as Flour, Bread now being packed over the mountains by the traders and I have no doubt but a great City will be started in the Carson Valley this spring. All its supplys must come direct from Sacramento City.

JULY 11TH. John Wethered sent for me having just returned from the diggings. John is quite badly poisoned, his face very much swollen and would not make his appearance on the street till I assured him that poison was so common here that any one would know what was the matter with him.[25] He looked as if he had been in a fine riot. He gave me such an account of the Rattle snakes in the mines as to satisfy me he had enough under present circumstances of mining.

Business here is improving, and I do hope I shall be able to remit to my friends what I borrowed to get here. Should be most happy to be the bearer of it. I think my time for making money ought to soon come.

The city is as healthy at present as was expected, diseases, dysentary & Fevers from one years end to another. I do hope I am acclimated. I try and take good care of myself in diet and free as possible from exposure after night, feel well at this time. They are now bringing snow in from the mountains or rather snow ice. They sell it by the waggin load to the Gambling Houses at one dollar per pound as fast as they can bring it in.

My love to Father, Brothers, Sisters, all.

FROM THY AFFECTIONATE SON
John Marsh Smith

[On the back of the folded letter]

July 12th have just received Sallys letter dated May 15/50
From E. Brooke-Gilly & Tommy 8/50
E. Brooke & Anne May 16
containing Sundrys all truly acceptable, the Neck Ribbons great treat as I have been trying to get one for two weeks

· · · · ·

Sacramento City, July 25 1850

To Elizabeth Brooke Smith
DEARE LIZZIE

I wrote thee by the steamer of the first, since when I have rec'd several letters from home, amongst them one from thee. It is a great source of pleasure to me to find thy letter written in such a pleasant and encouraging spirit and to find our dear little boys do not appear a trouble to our kind friends. I wrote Wm Talbot per steamer of 17th.

It is a great pleasure for me to think that ere this Fred is amongst you enjoying the comfort of home and Security of friends. It would have been utter folly for him to have remained here. He but seldom enjoyed good health, a blessing I fancy I am favoured with. I feel remarkably well. Business in this place is dull—and what helps make it worse for me, my partner has been down most of the time since our commencement with Fever. He is now in bed—and I am kept, owing to the circumstance, confined to the stove when I ought to be knocking around, but *such is life*.

I am thankfull I am not sick. Miners have done very poorly up to this time this year. Many are indebted to the traders who, owing to the fact of having their funds locked up, buy but sparingly. Many goods are now arriving out that have been shipped by capitalists at home who do not offer them for sale to the trade, but rent houses and retail them out to the traders and are satisfied with smaller profits than it has been customary to get here.

I sometimes think that California's juicy days are over. Judge Linch is dead, Law and order has been introduced, honesty can now hardly find space to concentrate a thought, and rascality receives the protection of the Court.[26] I have no doubt but there will be a very large business to be done here shortly, when I trust I may receive my share.

The overland Emigration is now coming in. They report great suffering for want of provision. A public meeting was held here last evening, and from the enthusiasm and deep feeling manifested against, abundance will soon be dispatched to the hungry. I know but little now to communicate. I heard some talk of a line of steamers to China. There is now a regular steamer to Oregon. The mail is in from the States. I have no doubt I shall receive a letter from thee. With love to all

FROM THY AFFECTIONATE
J M Smith

Kiss the little boys for me, give my love to all.

Ned Pearce
Jim Lea   all well
Ned Iddings

Jas Lea told me he intended writing his mother by this mail but he is now kept so constantly employed that he has no opportunity. His house is head quarters for all Missourians. I think Jim is making money.

• • • • •

Sacramento City, July 1850

To William Talbot
DEAR WILLIAM

I apologize for not writing you sooner but have been waiting for a streak of Luck (a great many people in this country are waiting for the same thing. Its hope on, and I reckon will be hope ever before all get their pile). Knowing the deep interest you feel in my welfare and the pleasure it would afford you should such at any time prove the case, but at present I see no speedy prospect of a windfall. Shall no longer delay a duty I owe a dear Friend or debar myself a pleasure for the lack of "Dame Fortune's smiles." (So its drive on Carter, for every dog must have his day, better luck next time is the motto of the individual citizen of a portion of the Globe that the American Eagle flies over. So whos a feard)

I have taken advantage of the very first opportunity to embark in Mercantile business. My partner is from N York. He's the son of Lambert Suydam, former president of the Union Ins Co of above mentioned place (And the number of our Ranch is Smith & Suydam, Sacramento City). We have been under weigh so short a time and business being generally dull that we can't give any flourishing acct of ourselves at this time, but I do not expect money to be made so fast here this fall as it was last, not only by a long shot. Many persons who have lately arrived amongst us from the States with money appear satisfied with smaller profits than it has been customary to obtain here, Say one hundred pr ct instead of from five to twenty, so a continued competition of this kind may soon reduce business here to a par with it at *home.*

I have no doubt ere this Fred Tyson has reached home. It would have been folly for Fred to remain here. Frequent spells of violent illness appeared his doom, and I shall be rejoiced to hear of his safe arrival home. Fred worked hard but had not the constitution to stand the peculiarities of the climate. Dysentarys and Fevers prevail here the year round, but I feel satisfied [that] with an increase of comforts health will become more general. I hardly think the sickness at present is of a dangerous character. My partner is down with the fever, which is of great disadvantage to us in our business operations. I feel remarkably well and try to take good care of my health. I had a pretty rugged time of it up to the time of my leaving the mountains in the winter, have been improving ever since and hope I am now acclimated. I hardly think I should have left the mines had it not been requisite on Fred's acct, but probably it is all best. I feel satisfied with having done so thus far and think my chance of making money is better here than in the mines.

I have within the last few days recd some letters from home (bearing the illness of Jas Atkinson and their youngest, ere this I hope they are well). I cannot post you in San Francisco affairs and hardly know what to conjer up. John Weathered stopped with me a couple of nights on his way to the diggings. His sojourn in the mines was of a very temporary character. Having been quite badly poisoned, he acted prudently by returning where remedys and advice are more profuse than in the mines and mountains of California. Some are very susceptible of poison while others roam with impunity amongst the innoculating shrubbery, proof against its sinus. John Weathered had some cards struck off here and distributed. He embarks in the Exchange Business of what is called at home, money Broker, and established himself in San Francisco.

Sacramento City is a singular place and grows as 'twere by magic. Last fall when I first arrived here it was in its infancy and but a few months previous New Helvetia on Sutters Embarcadero was only known by a trail crossing the river at this point traversed by Indians and mules, but now things wear a changed aspect. It is impossible for me to estimate the population but it amounts to thousands. Some fine and large brick warehouses have lately been completed.[27] The trader now is to be seen on the bank of the river, penciling on his memorandum book to find the net proceeds of his invoice just sold, but a little while ago his calculation would have been how to save his scalp. Merchandising and Gambling are the two principal occupations of the inhabitants here tho most Bankers in the last always the gainers. (Inhabitants almost universally full grown males.) Amusements, *Theatres*, night auctions, Bull fights, Bear dances, Cock fighting and Horse racing, and to complete the list I yesterday saw in the street for the first time an Organ Grinder with a monkey dressed in sold[i]er clothes dancing on the top of the music chest.

The face of the country around Sacramento is one vast plane. It is either plane or mountain in this country, there is no part I have been in moderately uneven, as one used to say at schole When we had that question in Geography, the face of the country, to answer. When in doubt I always found it a good guess but here it is rather flat or perpendicular.

The miners have not done well this season up to this time, but the rivers are falling and profitable mining must soon commence … [rest of letter missing].

• • • • •

Sacramento City, August 11 1850

To Nathan Tyson
Care of Tyson & Dungan
Baltimore, Md.
DEAR FATHER

I am in daily expectations of a letter from Frederick, giving account of his safe arrival at Panama. By the steamer just in, I have received dear Lizzie's letter of June 28 from Montgomery Co. I am thankfull to hear of the good health of you all and do hope our little boys may not prove an annoyance to you.

I took advantage of thy kind offer and drew on thee about the time Fred sailed for five hundred dollars. I invested that amount in Barley for the Sacramento Market, but unfortunately the vessel sunk in [word missing] Bay and all is a total loss as there is no insurance in this country and all is at the risk of the shipper. The heavy rates of rent, together with the high interest on money and the material deterioration in freight from last fall's rates, renders merchandising with limited means far from being lucrative. It is a universal complaint here, the inactivity of trade, a few large houses doing the bulk of the business, Persons having lately arrived amongst us from the States bringing assorted Stocks and goods and capital and seem[ing] disposed to reduce the rate of profit.

It will take me longer to accomplish my object in this country than I would desire as I have not the first outside shadow of a tie here. But rest satisfied, I shall do my best and take prudent care of myself, trusting the day may come when I shall be able to appear amongst you having accomplished the object of this my foreign mission. Sacramento, considering locality, maybe considered healthy at this time. There has been quite a large failure here within the last few days. Barton Lee, an Oregon man, who came here about 18 months since, probably penniless. His liabilities are something over one million dollars. Hundreds of men in the mines have their all in his hands. He called himself a banker and gave from 5 to 10% a month for all the money he could get on deposit.

The overland migration are coming in. They present a rather deplorable appearance and complain of the hardship they have suffered, and very many among them who have means sufficient to, go to San Francisco and start for home in the first steamer. The last steamer carried 350 passengers to Panama and refused 50 more besides. Large numbers of sailing vessels leaving full every few days. I can advise no shipments to this country, as large supplys are arriving from the English Colonies of the Pacific with an assurance that they can supply California with all she wants.

> With kindest regards to all
> FROM THY SON
> J. Marsh Smith

• • • • •

Sacramento City, August 12 1850
[Stamped] Sacramento 14 August 50 California

To Elizabeth Brooke Smith
Care of Matthew Smith
Baltimore, Md.
DEAR LIZZIE

Thy truly acceptable favour of June 23rd written from Walnut Hill has been recd by me.[28] It is a source of great comfort to me to find thee, our dear little boys, and Friends are blessed with health.

There is but little occuring here of interest. The mines are hardly paying for the labour that is being bestowed on them, rendering business dull in the extreme which is a universal complaint amongst all traders great and small. The citizens of this place are verry much disappointed that the present state of affairs should exist. I would never have settled in this swamp could I for one moment of imagined that such an inactive state of affairs would have taken the place of last years Bedlam in a business point of view. The overland emigration are coming in discouraged, haggard and without means. Many that have a sufficiency pass through here for San Francisco and take the first steamer to the States.

Say to Tony that I learn *Catherine* and *Laura Bevan* are both here, or rather in San Francisco, and I regret to say Candles are dull. I write today to Joseph Hobson requesting him to store them. I cannot account for their being so low as this place is almost bare of them, and they must, should ever business here assume anything of its last fall's character, command a price that will pay. I desire to give these shipments my personal attendance, and if I can so arrange it as to leave here for a few days will certainly do so. Say to Tony I left all the Bills of Lading & Invoices in hands of Cross Hobson & Co., should I not be in San Francisco to attend myself.

James Lea is doing a good business in the Hotel and frequently receives editorial puffs.

Boston *Ice* has become an article of retail traffic here and Ice carts are to be seen in the Streets so marked, price fifty cents per pound.[29] Lizzie, Kiss the little boys for me and tell them I want them to be good Boys and mind what is said to them. Say to Mother I would write her but I have nothing to communicate. Father endorsed on the back of the letter of 28th of June that my letter to Harriette has been recd. containing accts of Freds sickness in the Mines. Tell Harriet she must write me—Harriets letter is probably the first recd. I am verry much disappointed at not receiving a letter from Fred in Panama. I have no doubt he is home before this. Remember me to all.

FROM THY AFFECTIONATE
J. Marsh Smith

•　•　•　•　•

Ship Iona, Harbor San Francisco,
August 30 1850

To Elizabeth Brooke Smith
Care of Matthew Smith
Baltimore
Politeness of Joseph Hobson
DEAR LIZZIE

The heading of this will probably startle thee to know whats now out. Having been a little indisposed, my old doctor in Sacramento advised me to spend a few days at the Bay and take the Sea Air and I am now indebted to my kind friend Capt. James Hobson for the kindest care and best accommodation I have had since my sojourn in this land. I intend returning to Sacramento on Saturday next. The Captain says I am his patient and he is not going to let me leave him before Monday. He is truly kind to me and to all his acquaintances and is one of the best men in the world, and but a short time under his kind care, I feel sufficiently recruited to return to my business. I have given *Sacramento* a fair test, and it is but trifling with my health to settle down there with but poor remuneration in a pecuniary point of view and, I almost think, the vain hope of becoming proof against the Rivers of Sacramento Valley.

I wrote thee by the Steamer but regret I could not get off a dispatch to let thee know it was my intention to keep clear of Squatters fights, and am glad to say I was not in the conflict and felt no more excitement in the matter than I would to see the New Market and United Boys fight. The thing was a little Bloody and some fine men killed. Our Mayor is not dead but his recovery is doubtful. Doctor Brierly and Jessie Hambleton of Butte distinguished themselves in the fight. They were foremost in all the conflicts.

The heat of Sacramento is excessive, thermometer varying from 90 to 110 during the day, the nights pleasant. Business with us is in no means brisk and some heavy failures, and I fear more to follow. A vast many of the Miners have for months been engaged on turning the various rivers and banks, sanguine of success, living on the store keepers & traders who were compelled to demand credit of the Merchants to keep up supplys. Now the tale is about being un-folded [that] hundreds who would not have taken thousands of dol-lars for their claims have, after months of labour and toil, been able to test and found all was in vain, consider themselves broke and leave the store keeper and traders to whistle for their interest.

Dear Lizzie, I have recd many delightful letters that have been laying in Cross Hobson & Co. for some two or three weeks, from thee, telling of thy visit to Walnut Hill, from sister Anne, Belle, a letter from my Mother, one from Tony and another from thee Hand-ed me by Beverly Sanders, who seemed glad to see me.[30] Lizzie, thee cannot take my surprise when I met on the street Wm Robin-son. He is very anxious to get away from here as quick as possible, spent two nights on board of the ship with us, since when I have not seen him.

Yesterday was a holliday here, a Mock burial. Poor old General Taylor has been burried on the shores of the [word missing] and quite a solemn and remarkable a procession it was.[31] People of all nations composed the procession. These were *Masons, Soldiers, Fireman,* Foreigners and all sorts, amongst whom the Chinese were the most conspicuous from their great numbers and singular and rich dress. This San Francisco a most remarkable place. They are putting up large and elegant Brick Buildings such as would attract attention in a civilized land.

Joseph Hobson leaves in the steamer of the first for home, by whom I will send this letter. Feel so well I should leave for Sacra-mento today, but think I will stay that Joseph may tell you that he saw me at the latest date. Capt Hobson has just spoken to me to request me to send his respects. He says he does not know thee but thee is one of the Family. James Lea has been a little unwell but when I left Sacramento he was nearly well again. Ned Pearce was suffering some form of ague but not seriously indisposed. Ned Iddings and Sam Stark I think are both well. Say to all that think I ought to have written them that I have been away from my *Camp*. I don't want to call Sacramento my home. Hearing and seeing so much in this San Francisco I would not concentrate Ideas enough to serve all. I have Bill [Belle] and Annes kind letters in my pocket, for which I do thank them.

I have just had brought me a letter from Father Tyson which has been laying in office for a week, ought to have been delivered with the rest of Cross, Hobsons steamer letters but was not. I should have been sorry had it been lost. It is truly a very kind letter. Say to him I will write him by next steamer. The [piece missing] ship Fred went down to Panama is arrived there in [piece missing] thirty days from San Francisco, so reported. Suppose Fred must be safe home by this time. He did not write me. Say to Fred, the Mule Trade is dull in Sacramento. Fred was a regular jockey, he fully believed in Mule trading. Say to Fred a good many enquiries for him. Kiss the little boys. Recvd their note, Anne and Bell give most flourishing accounts of them. With kindest remembrances to all from

THY AFFECTIONATE HUSBAND
J M Smith

[On address side]

Dear Lizzie please reserve this sack of gold till I return

J M Smith

It is my own digging from Otter Creek about 3 oz in all.

·   ·   ·   ·   ·

To Nathan Tyson
care of Tyson & Dungan
Baltimore, Md.
DEAR FATHER

Thy kind favour of July 12 has been in hand but 2 weeks, having recvd it when on a visit to San Francisco. Having been a little unwell the doct advises me to spend a few days at the Bay which was of great service to me and had the pleasure of seeing Joseph Hobson on the morning of the day he sailed for the United States. I wrote Lizzie by him. I learned while down that the ship Fred went to Panama in had arrived after a good passage of 30 days and all aboard reported as well. I have recvd no letters from Fred yet from Panama, but he must now be with you to answer for himself.

The Squatter now has all seemed to subside and there is no excitement amongst us. I took no part with either side. Business is not to compare with last season. There is a vast overland emigration pouring in but they come exhausted of means and discouraged with the prospects. A vast number that are able to raise the funds take passage in the steamers for home perfectly satisfied with a short visit in this land. A majority of the claims in the Beds of the streams have proved, after months of severe toil and depravations to those engaged, failures. I think we may estimate nine out of ten. Some of these claims, so sanguine were people of their great wealth that from one to five thousand dollars has been offered and refused. A single individual claim, the traders, having equal confidence with the miners, have allowed them unlimited credit for provisions, so the Phantom of a General Bust rears his ugly form and stands sentinel over the Golden Gates through which thousands anticipated passing this fall laiden with the fruits of their labour *homeward Bound.*

Dear Father, I am obliged to thee for thy kind invitation to return, but I feel when I reach home as if I should never again want to leave it and as I am here in this country I had better try on for a while longer.

I feel satisfied I am to have good luck yet. I recvd yesterday a letter from Sister Belle enclosing one from Lizzie to Mother, I am rejoiced to learn Lizzie and the little Boys are so favoured with health as also the rest of you all. James Lea tells [that] the finest corn meal he has ever seen in this country was some of Tyson & Dungan put up in *tight* Brls. There are Mills no[w] grinding corn in this place, at Stockton and San Francisco, at this time keep up a fair supply, comes north about 4 cents meal, 8 cents per lb. It is always put up in Bags when ground here as it suits the packers better. My kindest remembrance to all. I shall write Lizzie.

THY SON AFFECTIONATELY

J. Marsh Smith

· · · · ·

Sacramento, Calif., September 11 1850

To Elizabeth Brooke Smith
Care of Matthew Smith
Baltimore, Md.
DEAR LIZZIE

Yesterday I rec'd Sister Belle's kind letter enclosing one from thee dated Walnut Hill July 22nd, written to Mother. I rejoice to find thee and the little Boys are so favoured with good health. Belle tells me she has had a glorious time at Cape May and that my Father, Mother, & Tony are amongst the visitors. I am rejoiced to find Father has taken some recreation. It will be of service to him and a great pleasure to Mother to have him along. I regret the proceeds of Tony's shipment for *Laura Bevan* will not reach him in time for his excursion to the Cape. The profits will not take him to France but might render him flush at Cape May.

When I last wrote thee I was on a visit to the Bay of San Francisco to enjoy the Sea Air. Was soon recruited. I staid on board of the *Iona*, a Magnificant ship, commanded by Capt Jas. Hobson who is the kindest man in California. I am well and was glad to report myself so when Joseph Hobson sailed. He goes to the States on business and to get married (probably he knows best). I sent per Joseph Hobson a little sack containing some gold of my own digging for thee, which hold on to till I return. I hope I will be rich enough to have it made up for thee & my friends. (I think I will have some luck yet—so keep up thy spirits. I know thee trys so to do.) Jas Lea is well. Ned Pearce, Stabler & Iddings, Doctor Brierly was verry conspicuous in the fight against the Squatters. I felt no inclination to embark in the enterprise, so thee must feel easy on my acct, All is now quiet.

I want very much to write to Belle & Anne, but really cannot find enough to [make] up an assortment for a decent letter. We have had quite a heavy rain here yesterday, which is [a] very remarkable thing in this country at this season. Business not brisk.

Lizzie, this is so poor an apology for a letter that I do not like to send it. I met in San Francisco Beverly Sanders. He appeared very glad to see me. I also met to my great astonishment Mr. Robinson. He was the Blueest Man I ever did see. I felt sorry for him. Kiss the dear little Boys for me, with love to all.

FROM THINE AFFECTIONATELY
J. Marsh Smith

[Pencil note]

Sept. 14th. I report myself well. There is a rumour in town of a tremendous large swamp of Gold having been found at Nevada, about 80 miles from this place. They are so in the habit of getting up false reports the day before the steamers leave for the states that I place but little faith in it. A chief of one of the Indian tribes here who has, as a chief under him, an Indian of the Delaware tribe, says tradition tells them that the Penn treaty was first broken by a White Man ordering two Indians to come down out of an apple tree. The Indians would not mind, and the white man shot them, then the Indians begun to hate, and sought revenge. I have sent Thos. M the [illegible] of exchange on acct of Tony's shipment to *Laura Bevan*.

• • • • •

Sch. *E.A. Spafford* at Sea, September 28 1850

To Elizabeth Brooke Smith
Care of Tyson & Dungan
Baltimore Md.
DEARE LIZZIE

In this country one becomes the creature of circumstance. In Sacramento I was not doing as well as one ought when the continued attacks of dysentary & Fevers were regular. I have a small Invoice of Goods as a Venture, and it is with the advice of many of my friends I make a trial of the Oregon markets. The Captain of the schooner is an acquaintance from Baltimore—a clever man, Capt. Beard.[32] We are bound to Astoria & Portland. We left the harbour of San Francisco at daylight this morning and are now at sea. This letter will be mailed by John Hooper, who accompanys the Captain to sea and returns by Pilot Boat.

Kiss the little boys.

> Love to all
> FROM THINE
> J. Marsh Smith

Say to Robert the drug business hardly presents an opening in San Francisco or Sacramento. I will see what can be done in that line in Oregon. I write this to let thee know where I am, shall if I do well return after more goods shortly. I will write Robert M.

> JMS *Remember me to all*

· · · · ·

[This letter was with that of November 19 1850, and the ensuing fragment, which was probably to Nathan Tyson.]

Shoal Water Bay, Oregon, October 21 1850[33]

To Elizabeth Brooke Smith

Dear Lizzie

After a rough passage of 22 days in a wrecked Condition and through stress of weather we once more find ourselves riding safely at anchor in the above mentioned Bay, about 20 miles to the N of the Columbia, which point we made yesterday one week since, but not being able to get a pilot were compelled to lay off and on. The weather all the time heavy and with a strong current setting to the North put us off in harbour, in which we now ride safe. There was no such harbour as the one we are now in laid down on the Captains chart. We were under the impression we were running into the Columbia, and by some of our passengers who had been in and out of the Columbia on several occasions the impression even after we got in judging from the different land marks, was perfectly satisfactory to them that we were in the Columbia—in fact they pointed out Astoria and Pacific City, and to top all we passed through breakers running by the chart of the Columbia soundings, corresponding with those laid down for the Columbia.[34]

We are not without company. We found a Brig from San Francisco that had been driven in, passed over the breakers having struck twice and been knocked down on her beam ends as often. She has 19 passengers and to our surprise, this morning we find anchored about 5 miles from us a schooner. No doubt they all think by seeing us here they are all O.K. The indians say we are one sun and one sleep to Astoria, and dreading passing over the breakers again in a sailing Vessel. Our passengers and the passengers of the Brig have hired two Indians to pilot us over to the Columbia into the white settlement. The waters of this bay abound in salmon and ducks of the finest kind. October the 15th was the worst predicament we were placed in.

To Elizabeth Brooke Smith
DEAR LIZZIE

I arrived from Shoal water bay just in time to see a friend as he was going down to California and request him to ask Abe Dungan to report me well. I had no opportunity to write thee but have written thee by the only opportunity that offered per Barque *Tarquina,* which letter may not reach thee by this day. Our vessel, the *E.A. Spafford,* after a hard time made her appearance in this port yesterday, being over 45 days from San Francisco, the goods I brought being most clothing are, I find, a dull article. I expected to do well with my return trade, *vegetables,* but a vessel has arrived since we left bringing gloomy accounts of the cholera which would make vegetables a risk. I am anxiously waiting for the Steamer to see what turn the disease has taken. If staying there, it will be most prudent for me to remain in Oregon till health favours San Francisco.

My last dates from thee is July 26th. I know there is quite a lot of letters for me at Cross Hobson & Co. How I should like to have them. It is now dull, raining. I do not know what to communicate interesting. Kiss the dear Little Boys for me. Remember me to all.

THINE AFFECTIONATELY
J. Marsh Smith

Commenced raining hard. We started their fires for them and then pushed on to Oregon City, distant about one mile, which we reached before all the supper in the city was wholly demolished, and fancy the Landlord would not call me a paying guest although I paid him his price. By invitation from McL I went with him to his store and spent the night with him.[35] Before we had retired his Father called down [*sic*]. (Dr. McL is, I should judge, a man of over seventy, in Size and personal appearance much like Mr. Henderson and a perfect Gentleman and a kind and amiable man. A Scotchman by birth and for more than Forty years in the service for the Hudson Bay Company and a great part of that time chief Factor for the same.

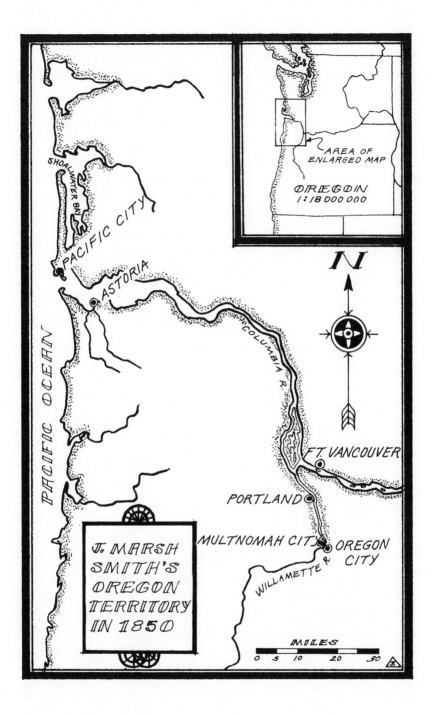

PACIFIC OCEAN

SHOALWATER BAY

PACIFIC CITY

ASTORIA

COLUMBIA R.

FT. VANCOUVER

PORTLAND

MULTNOMAH CITY

OREGON CITY

WILLAMETTE R.

J. MARSH SMITH'S OREGON TERRITORY IN 1850

AREA OF ENLARGED MAP

OREGON 1:18 000 000

N

MILES
0 5 10   20   30

He was pleasant and kind to me but I could not make anything out of him as he told me he had promised the command of his boat to someone else. I left Oregon City on Sunday morning at 10 o'clock in a whole boat and by Eleven I was again on board the *Spafford*.

P.S. I met some familiar faces in McL boat when I entered, in the shape of Candles and Soap with Smith and Curletts brand on. They composed a large portion of her freight and when encamped at night one of our Indians while setting round the fire drew from his breast a card which seemed to excite considerable interest amongst them. I felt a desire to see the Curiosity myself, when at my request they handed it to me and to my great Surprise it proved to be a business card of Tyson & Dungan and where they got it or how I know not. My kind regards to all. I will write Lizzie by next Steamer.

AFFECTIONATELY YOUR SON
J. Marsh Smith

If I succeed in getting the river boat, I will get it on Shares on half the profit of leasing half the expense.

J.M.S.

•   •   •   •   •

Portland, Oregon, November 1 1850

To Elizabeth Brooke Smith
DEAR LIZZIE

I wrote thee a letter and handed to pilot on leaving the Bay of San Francisco. This point is the destination of our vessel, but owing to misfortunes of various kinds we were driven in to Shoal water bay about 40 miles to the North of the Columbia. Not liking to risk the vessel until some more substantial repairs could be put upon her than the conveniences of Shoal Water Bay afforded, with some Fort passengers we started with an Indian guide for the settlement, which after travelling one and a half days we made, Pacific City opposite to Astoria being the point we made. After spending the night at the former place, we crossed over to Storia and took passage in a small steamer for this point.[36] Portland is on the Wilhammet about 12 miles below Oregon City and a growing place, contains probably about a hundred houses and is probably the greatest business point at this time in the territory.[37]

I have just learned that the commanding officer at Fort Vancouver has employed a pilot and sent relief to the captain of our schooner, and if she has not been too badly abused I may soon hear of her safe arrival in the river with my little stock of merchandise, having made a little raise through the kindness of my Brother Robert, who authorized me to make use of a part of some funds he might have in the hands of Cross Hobson & Co., which I have done to the amount of seven hundred dollars. I am now in hopes daily of hearing from the supercargo who left at Astoria of the safe arrival of the vessel in the river. If they cannot get her out I will have to go over and do the best I can. The Indians are peacable and quiet but no money amongst them.

I send this letter to be mailed at San Francisco by a sailing vessel which leaves here tomorrow. I had no opportunity to write thee from Astoria by the mail steamer as she was nearly ready to leave when I got along side of her, but sent word by an acquaintance who was going down to California to tell Abe Dungan to get some one to report me well. I will try and write Robert M by the Mail Steamer. Dear Lizzie, I did not leave California for Oregon for the purpose of getting farther from home, but having had a succession of misfortunes in my trading operations, I thought a change for the better might be the result and then I would be sooner with you. Direct my letters as usual to Cross, Hobson & Co. If I find I can make the trade profitable between here and California, I shall stick to it. Say to Robert I will write him and give him my views. I do not believe there is a drug establishment in this whole territory. A regular drug house on a small scale keeping a supply of Paints and oils would do well.

There is a large emigration daily arriving here from the States and from California. Portland at present is headquarters for trade but there are a good many towns springing up all along the Wilammett. Oregon City is a small place and will always be a manufacturing and milling point, but it will never be the great place as shipping cannot approach within some miles of it.

Kiss the dear little boys. Tell them to be good and give no one trouble. With love to all.

FROM THINE AFFECTIONATELY
J. Marsh Smith

· · · · ·

Portland, December 2 1850

To Elizabeth Brooke Smith
DEAR LIZZIE

The Steamer *Gold Hunter* arrived here yesterday and I learn leaves here tomorrow for San Francisco. The *Spafford* I am still on board of and have not yet disposed of all my traps. The steamer brings the acceptable intelligence that the Cholera has abated in California. I intend going down in the Schooner. We will probably not leave (Oregon) in less than 3 or 4 weeks and will be late in January or sometime in February before we get to San Francisco, when I hope to receive a treat in the way of letters. My last dates from thee sometime in July. The articles I brought up here have not paid me well. I trust to the vegetables I take down to make on.

I have not time to say much as I have just got down from the vessel. She lays about two miles higher up the river than Portland and the boat is [a]bout leaving for her. The steamer that has arrived was unexpected or I would have had time to write thee with more care. I want to write Brother Robert, to thy Father, to Mother, but have not now the chance. Say to Robert M. that there is not a regular drug House in all Oregon Territory and that a regular establishment with a well selected assortment of Glass, Oils & Paints, dyes & co. would pay well if he should see fit to establish a house. The selection at this point might be left till his goods arrive in the Territory. Portland is at this time the most flourishing town in the Territory but many are striving for this ascendancy so it is hard to tell what will be the best point in a few months.

Give my love to all. Kiss the dear little Boys tell them to be good.

FROM THINE AFFECTIONATELY
J. Marsh Smith

Excuse the rough workmanship on this epistle

Notes to Chapter Two

1. Bond may have been sent to San Francisco as a representative of his firm. Evidently he left Baltimore before JMS's letter of December 1849 could have reached him.
2. JMS addressed both his father and his father-in-law in this way.
3. On the American River, approximately three miles from Sacramento, Fort Sutter's was the home of John A. Sutter, whose associate, John Marshall, is credited with finding gold while constructing a lumber mill 40 miles upriver.
4. Grandmother Ellicott was Lizzie's mother, Martha Ellicott Tyson (1795-1873).
5. Near Coloma.
6. Possibly William High, aged 27, born in Virginia.
7. Possibly Thomas Scott, aged 24, born in Virginia.
8. Near Georgetown.
9. Built in 1850 by Nathan J. Stevens and operated by him until his death in 1857.
10. Now Ellicott City and a suburb of Baltimore, Ellicott Mills was the family home of Martha Ellicott Tyson.
11. Ned Pearce, of Brickhead-Pearce, Baltimore, who brought JMS mail sent in care of Cross, Hobson, left the mines on May 14 1850, as did High and Iddings.
12. Near Mormon Island and at the mouth of the Feather River, Vernon was a depot for goods and transport. It is now submerged by Lake Folsom.
13. Dover's powder was made from ipecac, opium and lactose or potassium sulphate.
14. Lizzie's grandfather, Elisha Tyson, was a staunch prohibitionist who refused to allow the storage of whiskey in his warehouses.

15. A general trading vessel built in 1849 by William H. Webb and owned by Tucker, Cooper & Company of New York.

16. Evans gained considerable notoriety in the Eastern press for his claims of being among the first to find gold in California.

17. Lambert Suydam was president of the Union Insurance Company of New York. James Suydam was associated at various times with a number of business enterprises in Sacramento.

18. Unclaimed goods were auctioned in San Francisco for shipping costs, thus providing a relatively inexpensive means of starting a business in Sacramento.

19. This method made unloading and warehousing unnecessary.

20. Isabelle Tyson, a sister of Lizzie, born March 17 1823; Lucy Tyson, Lizzie's youngest sister, born March 20 1833.

21. The TransIsthmus Railroad was fully operating by 1855. For mention of the railroad survey, see Appendix.

22. It was customary to "take the waters" at Bedford, Pennsylvania, the site of White Magnesia Springs (information courtesy of Judge Clark).

23. Mary Marsh Smith, a sister of JMS, born October 14 1823; Sarah R. Smith, a sister of JMS, born April 5 1830; Catherine Ellen Smith, JMS's youngest sister, born September 14 1831

24. The torrential rains often prevented many delegates from attending the first legislative session, which at times moved from San Jose to Monterey and Sacramento. JMS's speech in Sacramento was doubtless against slavery, a tense subject as California appealed for statehood. The two senators elected as first order of business were the popular John C. Frémont, a Whig, and William M. Gwin, a pro-slavery Democrat.

25. John Wethered was certainly suffering from poison oak (rhus toxicodendron).

26. The lynch law was prevalent during the squatters' riots that ended in the summer of 1850 with the establishment of law and order.

27. Many of these warehouses have now been restored, re-creating the appearance of Sacramento in 1850.

28. Presumably in Montgomery County, Maryland (see JMS's letter of August 11 to Nathan Tyson), where Ellicott Mills was.

29. Ice, packed in sawdust, was a regular New England export in the 19th century.

30. A friend of the Smith family from Baltimore, Beverley Saunders eventually became a business partner of Abe Dungan in San Francisco.

31. President Zachary Taylor died on July 10 1850, but the news did not reach San Francisco until the arrival of the United States mail steamer on August 24.

32. Captain Edward (Ned) Beard, master of the *E.A. Spafford* and later of the *Merchantman* and the *George and Martha*, evidently considered himself a concerned friend of JMS (see Beard's letter to JMS of February 28 1851). He was lost at sea in 1853.

33. Shoalwater Bay, in the Oregon Territory, is now Willapa Bay, Washington, just north of the Columbia River.

34. Pacific City was on Baker's Bay on the north shore of the Columbia River, separated from the ocean by Cape Disappointment, near the present Fort Canby.

35. Dr. John McLoughlin ("McL") had retired in 1846 from his position as Chief Factor of the Hudson's Bay Company at Fort Vancouver and moved to the Territorial capital, Oregon City.

36. Astoria, or "Storia," named after John Jacob Astor, is near the mouth of the Columbia River on the south shore.

37. Wilhammet: Willamette River.

CHAPTER THREE
1851

. . . . .

To Elizabeth Brooke Smith
DEAR LIZZIE

I have just arrived here from Oregon, came down in the Barque *Louisiana* twelve days from Astoria. It is now late in the evening and will write further by next steamer.

I am ranching out at Abe Dungans, who desires to be remembered to thee. I have seen Bob George & George Gibson.[1] Walked up and spent the evening with them and was highly delighted at the recpt [receipt] of the *degarrs* of our dear little boys.[2] Trust they may be favoured with the health they appeared to be blest with when they sat for their pictures. I prize very much the little bundle Thee sent me. Thank the girls for their kindness. I have not yet got all my letters—I hear of some I must have in the morning. Have gathered enough to learn of your good health, which is a source of great happiness for me, and one from Fred satisfying me of his safe return home. I met quite unexpectedly with T. Butler King on the street this afternoon—he told me he had met my sister and my brother at Mr. Corwins. He gave me a kind invitaiton to call on him, which I shall do.

I see I have been appointed Naval officer for the Port of San Francisco but then again, I ain't. Dear Lizzie, I excuse thy mistake. I know thy anxiety—I could not but help smiling when I [read] the sentence. I thought it was too rich a b[e]rth to fall to my share, and as for anything in Sacramento, don't be *afraid, I ain't there,* and rejoice I left it when I did. Tony says something about Marshall of lower California that is not exactly the thing, but as I am numbered in the [blank space] of Oregon and expect to return there, I should like Thomas M to enquire of Mr. Corwin if he thinks there is an opening for a young man. I am at my countrys service. My reasons for mentioning this particular berth are these—

ıst Oregon is a *human* country. It has high mountains and Steep cataracts, its climate salubrious—all interesting, and the latter particularly so to one who has spent some time in the Sacramento Valley. Its lands are productive, its timber gigantic, its *saw* mills numerous, and I feel satisfied its Gold Mines are rich. Its rapid progress is certain, and further, this said deponent states that if present prospects should not be frustrated (which if they are he will look upon it as his luck), he will try his chance there in trade—and my object for accepting this office of Marshall for the Territory, were I to get it, would be if Merchandising was not paying, that I might have a berth by which to raise salary enough to make home in the fall. I would not sacrifice a mercantile business for an office if it was or should be paying, and I think it would throw chances in one's way that he would not be likely to meet with as a secluded citizen. Say to Father and Mother I am no political aspirant but want to do all I can for what I think is best calculated to hasten my return, dearest Lizzie, once more amongst you.

Love and kind remembrances to all. I want to write to Robert. Say to him his candles are all sold at saving prices, and will make remittance by next Steamer. Was under the impression that Cross, Hobson and Co. had done so till today. Segars, say to him, like all else in California, is dull, but I think I can make these pay which he has shipped. They will certainly not loose anything. I will retail them first. They have not yet arrived. Lizzie, thee will excuse this scrawl. If there was time I would copy and correct. Kiss the dear little Boys.

FROM THINE AFFECTIONATELY

J. Marsh Smith

P.S. I must write Gilley. I don't like spinning him any yarns to excite his curiosity. I want our little boys to imbibe no disposition to wander.

. . . . .

San Francisco, January 22 1851

To Catherine Marsh Smith
Care of Mathew Smith
Sharp & Co. [?]
Baltimore
DEAR MOTHER

Thine of Dec 9th was handed me by Mr. Moore.[3] I wrote thee and Father while in Oregon, but presume owing to some faults of the public carrier that the letter has been delayed. I note thy kind invitation to return, and assure thee it will be a joyous day to me when the time arrives, truly trusting that Lizzy and again all will try and make yourselves happy on my acct. I do really believe my health to be better than it has been for months, and have come down here for the purpose of trying to get a stock of Goods such as will suit the Oregon market. I think I shall succeed, but most unfortunately for me those who are the least able are the ones most disposed to give me a lift.

I have made acquaintances in Oregon who will be of service to me if things turn out there this summer as is anticipated by the knowing ones. Good Gold diggings have been discovered in Oregon and large numbers of people are leaving the California mines and striking for the mines of Oregon, whose mining districts are believed to be both productive and healthy, and should the rush be to the Oregon mines this summer, and I fixed some where on the Columbia or Wilhamette, my chance will be as good as some others and better than in California, as I have the promise of being let into the secrets of speculators and a promise of assistance and means, from a success that I feel satisfied can be depended on.[4]

I do not know how it is, but upon reflection I find my acquaintance there pretty large. I do not know how it is I missed getting acquainted with the Governor,[5] but on reflection I recollect having had an invitation from a Gentleman to accompany him on an evening visit, but was debarred that pleasure owing to the high price of Boots. The only pair I owned being rather too weighty a matter to introduce into the Parlor of so high a Functionary. I met with T. Butler King on the street. He gave me a kind invitation to call him, which I done, but as he was setting over his wine, I left the ranch, to call again. I think he will be sent to the United States Senate.

I am glad I left Sacramento when I did. There has been a great deal of sickness there and a poor business done. I have no desire to return to it. I should like, if it can be done and a change is to be made, to get the Marshal Ship for Oregon, But between thee and myself, I would not accept it if I am so fortunate as to do tolerably well at trading, but if the appointment is to be had, I want it so that if I should be dissapointed in trade, I may be able to realize enough from that office to pay expenses home, where I hope to be in the fall. Love to Lizzie and all.

THY AFFECTIONATE SON,
J. Marsh Smith

•　•　•　•　•

San Francisco, January 29 1851

To Elizabeth Brooke Smith
Care of Tyson and Dungan
Baltimore, Maryland
DEAR LIZZIE

I have since my arrival here been favoured with numerous acceptable favours from home. Owing to some delay you have not recvd by my last dates per Mr. Moore any letters from me while in

Oregon. I wrote frequently, met with a good deal of kindness, am predjudiced in favor of the country, believing it to be far superior to N. California in every respect save its mineral wealth, which has just begun to develop its self, and even in this respect think it will equal it. I assure thee I have not seen anything to infatuate me so since I left our home as to induce me to believe that under the most flattering circumstances thee and our little Boys could be as happy here as amongst those who are so kind and dear, I never could.

I expect to return shortly to Oregon, anticipating a result there in the state of affairs, speculative at present but this far as it were maturing to my satisfaction. I hold on to a stubborn kind of hope that my plans are not always to be frustrated, and if Oregon turns out to be rich in Gold I do think that I have found stronger friends who will furnish me means to operate with, they assure me so at least. I do wish to be so fortunate as to be able to return to thee in the fall with a sufficiency to place me out of debt and on one hundred and fifty acres of Good land near home. Persons have retired without a light ahead and in the morning have shaped their course without a dollar to steer by, and in less than a month have made more than I would stop in this country another month to double (but its still down on Carter, better luck next time, hope on hope ever).

I am anxiously expecting letters from Oregon but will not receive them by the first steamer that is to arrive. There are now three running between there and this place. I met Mr. King on the street, he kindly invited me to call on him, which I did, but was not able to see him as he was dining. The next day he left for San Jose where he has been ever since. I will see him on his return. I shall get Mr. King to write to Mr. Webster and some of my other friends will write other partys and I will write Mr. Corwin and Thomas M.[6] I want the Marshal Ship for Oregon. (If I should get it and am doing well I will not accept, but merely want an anchor ahead.) From all I can gather there is nothing in the Custom House left here.

I received Anne & Bells Kind letters, also Father Tysons. I want to answer them all but have nothing to say at present. Everything in California is *dull, dull, dull.* Look out for General *bust, bust, bust.* I think he will be about shortly. My advice to my friends is, keep your Money and your goods where you can control it and then yourselves. This is a country where *honesty* is a phantom too hideous to be countenanced. It has some martyrs, though. Love to all. I hope to be with you in the fall.

THY AFFECTIONATE HUSBAND
J. Marsh Smith

Kiss the dear little Boys for me. Tell Gill I noticed he had on a jacket with brass buttons and trousers and Brother Tommy looked first rate with his little frock on. Their pictures were truly acceptable. Tell the girls to write me often. I will try to reply.

J.M.S.

Jan 31st Mr. Ober of Ober and McConky has kindly offered to take for me a degar, so yesterday I sat for one. Accompanying it is one I had taken on my arrival from the Mines last summer.[7] I was not well at the time it was taken, and thought I would, when I got first rate have a *Genteel* one taken, and now forward both. The one taken last Summer just from the mines was pronounced first rate at the time it was taken, and my friends say the one I had taken yesterday is as good as could possibly be taken of a person. I feel better and more like myself than I have since I left home.

THINE AFFECTIONATELY
JMS

. . . . .

Astoria, Oregon, February 21 1851
[Postmark] Astoria Or Mar 24

To Elizabeth Brooke Smith
Care of Tyson & Dungan
Baltimore, Md.
DEAR LIZZIE

We have arrived here all safe in Ten Days from San Francisco. Night before last we laid to in a severe gale of wind off the Mouth of the river but rode it out without the loss of a single rope yarn, and once more I am safe inside the Columbia bar.

It is, Lizzie, my intention to return home this fall, and as no inducements offered to remain in San Francisco I was Glad to leave it. Mr. King probably might have given me an inspectors berth in the custom house but *ship fever*, the disease of California, and other serious objections make it a poor situation. In Astoria here they tell us that there is great excitement in the upper country in regard to the Klamouth Mines. They say they are richer than any mine in California, *dare be* people have arrived who have had great success and large partys are prepairing to leave for diggings.

I write, Lizzie, to let thee know of my safe arrival and that I really think my health is first rate and I weigh more than I did when I left home. My average weight in California last Winter & Summer & Fall was 130 lbs., since my first visit to Oregon, 149 to 152 lbs. I want to consult with one or two friends here before I become fixed.

Kiss the dear Little Boys. Tell them to be good. With love to all

FROM THY AFFECTIONATE
J. Marsh Smith

I want my claim for the Marshalship of this Territory to be remembered by you.

JMS

• • • • •

Astoria, February 28 1851

To John Marsh Smith
on board Barque *Luisanna*
Columbia River or Portland
US
DEAR SMITH

On my arrival here, I was informed that you were on board of the *Luisana*. I am sorry I did not see you. I understand that you were going in business here in Oregon. If you do, I sincerely hope you will make a fortune, Smith. If there is anything I can do for you in S. Francisco write me and I will do it with pleasure. If you have any letters for me just direct them to S. Francisco drop me a line down here as it is uncertain when I shall leave here. Let me know all the news, I expect to be back here in about 6 weeks from the time I leave Astoria. Mr. Burns will be pleased to see you,[8] dont forget to call on the family and give them my kindest respects.

Your Sincere Friend
Edward H. Beard

. . . . .

Portland, Oregon, March 9 1851

To Elizabeth Brooke Smith
Dear Lizzie

I wrote Thee from Astoria noting my safe arrival, and as a mail will leave here tomorrow for San Francisco I take advantage of the opportunity to pen Thee again. On my arrival here I found things very much as I anticipated. The mania here is Lo for the Klamouth Mines. The Male portion of the community are fast leaving, and even at this early approach of Spring and before the hills have shed their mantle of Snow, individuals are arriving in the settlement who report the Road to the diggings to be good for Waggons to within fourty miles of the mines. This fourty miles at this season, they are compelled to pack on Mules and Horses and some who have returned are packing back heavy Stocks of Goods from this and various points along the Willamette. Twice I tried the Mines and as often found myself defeated. Having lost some faith of growing rich by gold digging, I feel but little curiosity to try my luck in that line and particularly as I am encouraged to believe there is something better left for me.

Thee must, dear Lizzie, try and keep in good cheer and by thy letters I believe thee does. Time speeds on, and if life and health are mine in but a few months more I trust I shall be with you all. Although, Lizzie, I am far from home I hardly feel amongst strangers. I do not like San Francisco, but I think from present impressions I may have to go down for a short time, and as beggars cant be choosers I must do the best. I made some good purchases for a friend of mine in this Territory while in San Francisco and he seems well pleased. I had a short talk with him. We are to have another, I think the result will most probably be good, in my next further particulars.

I am well, Kiss our dear little Boys for me, tell them to be good. Love to all, I want to write Belle and Anne. No doubt ere this you have recd my two degares. I always try and carry mine with me, I treasure them so much. Beverly Saunders promised to get Mr. King to write a letter for me to Washington. He (Mr. King) was at San Hosa when I left and I came off without having a talk with him.

THINE AFFECTIONATELY

J. Marsh Smith

. . . . .

Portland, Oregon Territory, March 21 1851

To Elizabeth Brooke Smith
Care of Matthew Smith
Baltimore, Md
DEAR LIZZIE

I write knowing thy anxiety to hear from me. I have but little to say. Thankful to report myself well, as Thee may judge from the fact that I weigh one hundred and fifty two pounds, While my Sacramento standard was one hundred and thirty. I find things here in an unsettled state. All depends upon one thing. If it proves easier to transport Goods from the valley here than from San Francisco, affairs in Oregon will undergo a great change.

I look anxiously toward returning to thee soon, and trust I may meet with some success ere long. Things here will not fully develop themselves for a month or two.

I learned but a few moments ago there would be a chance of sending this to the mouth of the river to connect with the mail for California, and as the boat is about leaving I close with a desire to be remembered to all. Send love for thee, a kiss for our little Boys. Say to Robt M. there is quite a fine drug establishment just gone into operation.[9] There is not much for them to do just at present. He wrote me enquiring of Doct. Massy, I learned nothing of him. Young

Fendall I learn is farming Some where above Oregon City. A person told me he saw him a week since and he was well. I am expecting some letters from San Francisco as I left word how to forward to me. Thee direct as usual.

Electioneer for me, as the Marshalship here I think will be worth having. Should I be so lucky as to make sufficient to pay expenses and my debts at home I will be a most happy man. I am in as good spirits as tis possible for one to be who is so far away from all that is so dear to him. Lizzie, when I get home I wont want to leave *any more*. There has been but one mail from San Francisco this month, it brought me nothing.

FROM THINE AFFECTIONATELY
J. Marsh Smith

• • • • •

Portland, Oregon, April 4 1851

To Elizabeth Brooke Smith
DEAR LIZZIE

As there is a mail to leave tomorrow morning at 5 o'clock I take advantage of the chance to write Thee. There has been a good deal of rain falling here lately, but for the last few days we have been favoured with occasional Sun Shine. Today it has changed to rain and now falls fast. I am anxiously waiting the arrival of the mail in hopes of hearing from thee.

The mass of the People have left the Settlement here and gone to the Mines, we are hearing news from that region. In anticipation of large demand for supplys for the mining district of Oregon, large stocks of Goods have been shipped from San Francisco which, together with the arrivals direct from the States and no demand for goods, has created a Glut in the market and all are complaining bitterly of dull times and poor returns. If the mines prove good, prospects here will brighten. I was induced to return here thinking things would be very prosperous and believing I had found a friend who had means that I could secure the use on joint acct, but trade here presents such a dull prospect and its revival depends upon circumstances which are yet to develop themselves. I do not feel at liberty to advise or risk on an uncertainty the money of a man who has toiled hard and places every confidence in my integrity.

I will enclose thee a letter* from him recd a day or two since from him. The person I have allusion to is the same that I made purchases for when in California and fortunately for me, or rather for my judgement, all the articles I bought him paid very handsomely, while some he bought without my advice still hang and daily, I suppose, judging from his character, pronounces [blank space] upon them. He merely bought on speculation, is not engaged in any business nor never has been a mercantile kind, and I am merely hanging on in hope the mines may turn out well and the trade concentrate here or Oregon City. If it does, from what my friend Burns tells me I think I can depend on him for a start. If it turns out that they can draw supplys from some more convenient source, my *cake* will be *dough*, as there will be no business to do here of any consequence this summer.

I think often of Thee and our little boys and numerous friends, and if it were possible to increase in my attachment could in truth say that absence makes the heart grow fonder. I am looking for my friend Burns down every day, when I will have a talk. Kiss our dear little Boys, love to all.

I am well
FROM THINE
J. Marsh Smith

. . . . .

*Possibly the following from Hugh Burns, dated February 6, which would have been forwarded by Joseph Hobson.

Portland, February 6 1851

To John Marsh Smith
to the care of Cross Hobson & Co
San Francisco
FRIEND SMITH

I have just come and find that my friend Neall has gone down to King & Cross and will get on the *Sea Gull* thair. I thearfore send the Gold dust to the amount of $2144.80 by Todd & Co. Mr. Todd come up with me in the *Oregon* to see what he could do in the Express Business in Oregon, so I send the money by him. I paid him one percent for freight and Insurance, he is to deliver it to H.Q. Adams and Mr. Adams will pay to Lowenstein & Gibson & Co. and to the French man and the Balance he will pay over to you.

Mr. Todd had a letter for you that he will leave at Cross & Hobson Co for you. In that I told you what to buy for me. If you see a Good bargon in some other things that you know will sell here, why, you buy them either for me or for you and me together. Cigars is very dull here at present, so is chees and crackers. Shuger is seling at 13 cts wholesale, Coffee 22cts yet. If you can get some good coffee not above 14cts, Buy it, Good green tea also is cheap. Send me up a few small cask of good Brandy and some good porter or ale if cheap. In my other lerter [letter] I told you to buy doors and windows. Get as many good 4 or 6 panel doors inside and out as you can. I think by this time they are cheap. I forgot the tin of cake at the Thoms Bennett that Mr. Gibson brought down for me. If you find it send it to me altho it wont set here, but I will eat but one.

Capt. Beard is well, he commenced loading yesterday. In 12 hrs he will be of[f]. He has not seen the Girll yet. I will as soon as I can get a little more time write to you and give you a full account of all that is going on here.

Write to me and let me know how you are doing and when you will come up.

Give my best to Mssrs Lowenstein & Gibson Co., to Mr. Dungan and to all my old friends. If you see Capt Hoit, rember me to him and tel him that we would like to see him up here with a good light steam boat that could run on the rapids. From your friend and well wisher.

H. Burns

. . . . .

San Francisco, March 22 1851

To John Marsh Smith
DEAR JOHN

Enclosed herewith four letters which I found at Cox room of C.H. [Cross, Hobson].*

I arrived here a month ago and left our family all well in the states in January last. I met your wife and sister in law at our Fathers, The former anxious about you and eager to join you here or at home. I offered to bring her out to you. Tom wishes you to return, as better than making nothing abroad, and I would recommend you to go *in case you have no certain and permanent as well as profitable employment.*

Let me hear from you. I learn that you are at Portland from Mr. Dungan and, agreeable to his direction, send this to care of Norris & Co. there. The mail Steamer *Panama* came in yesterday with date to 15 February but letters not yet delivered.

My wife with Mr. Main and *his* wife and Mrs. Captain are all here and send their regards & I remain very truly yr. friend.[10]

Jos. Hobson

. . . . .

*See preceding letter from Hugh Burns. The other letters have apparently not survived.

To John Marsh Smith
FRIEND SMITH

John handed me the 28 yours of the same date and I regret very much that you have met with such a loss in the stores. By this mail I received letters from B Lowenstein & Gibson. Mr. Adams has paid them and has sent me the ballance of the mony. By their Bill the Sandwich Island shugar is corect, but the manilla they say is 12341 by my account it is 12049. The account of sacks are corect, but the damaged state in which [they were] delivered accounts for the diference—48 sacks, White Crash shugar—3220.

My account 3061, the balenc [balance] lost out of bad sacks. They say by the short account of the Manilla shuger that when they bought it from Mr. Bond he told them that he had 20,000 lbs of it but has now showen them the oregonal invoice and that they can attach no further blame than that of an oversight of him in the matter. I supose they would like if Oregon had a good many such fools as me to let them have mony and then pay them five percent per mounth to Boot, but we will see about it. If Shuger fell it would then get 20,000 lbs. They send me the invoice of their stationary, carpeting & oil cloth with the bill of prices of the carpeting and cloth. If you think any person in Portland wants to purchase any of it, I will send you down the invoice & bill, they propose to set 50 per ct. above cost. They wish me to rem[em]ber them to you. If you write to them I wish you would state to them the condition the shuger came in. I have nea[r]ly sold out, and if the weather was good, I would have closed out before this.

How is friend Barnhart coming on.[12] Tel him to let me know if he can sell crackers or segars, if-so, will send him down some. Friend Smith, what are you doing or what do you wish to do, and if i can help you let me know your plans and what you think you would like to do and if I can help you I will do it willingly, so let me know what you would like to do. What are thare in Portland that can be bought cheep. I may go down this week.

YOUR FRIEND
H. Burns

• • • • •

San Francisco, April 4 1851
[Postmark] Astoria, Oregon, April 8

To John Marsh Smith
Portland, Oregon
DEAR JOHN

Your form of 21st March have been received and contents noted.

The *Silas Richards* has arrived and will discharge in a day or two. I will receive your segars, and hold them until I hear from you, there is little or no demand for them and are selling at about cost. Please let me hear from you by return steamer.

I am no longer a partner in the large Commercial House of D.M.&P. [unidentified] and on the day Mr. M & P put their names to a document declaring the independence of A.S.D. that individual in company with his friend W.B. celebrated the event by dining together and getting most dreadfully tight. I have since that time my dear fellow been in high spirits and hope to make some money.

You know exactly the state of my finances, and would say if you can make arrangements with Burns to send some money down so I can use it for you in the purchase of goods for your markets. I would do so but if you cannot, send me a list of what you will have and I will try to buy them on joint a/c/. What have those vessels in that have arrived in your port.

Hams Prime in Market	15¢
Lard	12
Butter	30
Oysters Fresh	16
Candles Sperm	42-45
Soap	12¢
Brandy American	1.50-1.75
Whiskey	1.50
Ale & Porter	3.50
Lemon Syrup	3.50-4.00

In writing for foods be explicit as Jas Hobson has not sent us your letters. I enquired for them be he preferred sending them himself, hoping the news from home may be pleasing to you.

I remain very truly
YOUR FRIEND
A.S. Dungan

• • • • •

San Francisco, April 22 1851

To John Marsh Smith
Care of Messrs Norris & Co
Portland, Oregon Ty
DEAR JOHN

I was very much gratified at receiving your letter of 10 April, as I had heard from those with whom you have been corresponding that you were not much given to chirography and I need not be surprised at not having my letters answer'd[13]

It seems you are disappointed in your expectation of doing business in Oregon. You and Burns, from whom we have two letters of like dates with yours, speak in equal terms of the poor prospect of business in Oregon: of there being no money in the country; no men to buy, all having gone to the mines,[14] and plentiful stocks of goods both by importation from San F. and direct from the States. I must believe it, tho' it's against the grain to do so, that what you and he state is correct and I am mightily sorry of it. I calculated on Oregon taking away some of our overgrown stocks and thereby helping us out of the scrape but there appears to be no hope on any side. From every quarter we have and have had news only of overstocked markets, low prices and dull prospects and on top of it all nearly 100 vessels have come in lately with large assorted cargoes from the States, England and Germany. What's to be the upshot of things, I don't know, yet our mkt. has not wavered. In fact we have been doing a larger business since these arrivals than before and generally at better or at least no worse prices. Larger arrivals of people from the States via Isthmus are taking place. The *Republic* brought up 430 of whom 40 were women and 60 children!!!! What a baby-dom the cabin must have been, and she brings news that 1,500 had arrived at Chagres by late steamers. I suppose we'll find room to stow them away somewhere. For my own part, if we manage to stick together and hold our own, clearing only our most economi-cally administered expenses, I shall be satisfied for 12 months yet. I am no advocate of change—and rather depend on perseverence and proper management in a fixd deportment of business than on the chances of more satisfactory returns from a change.

The Soap affair is rather exploded. I could not find a man compe-tent to undertake the management of it and I can hardly agree with you that it requires no skill. I have gleaned some considerable in-formation from Merc's [?] Dictionary but just enough to convince me that it would be futile to attempt the manufacture without a person of experience to superintend it. So until such an individual turns up Soap Manufacture must be at a stand still, as far [as] I am concerned. Burns can hardly complain of our charging him interest on any of the money he left to pay for Sugar with. We paid it over immediately to Hussey, Bond & Hale and only had it returned to us when the Sugar was wghd. In the mean time several other transac-tions occur'd by which Burns became indebted to us in general acct. and on these items we charged interest. As far as we were con-cerned in the Suger Money, we had no use of its further than paying it over immediately to them—and could not therefore be expected to allow interest. The Sugar was doubtless in as fair order as Man-illa Sugar generally is. It was more-over rec'd by Burns' agents and as it passed their inspection, we should be exonerated. Burns writes us in a slightly complaining strain but on the whole appears pretty well satisfied. It would have been far better for him if he had or-dered us to sell here when Sugar had advanced so much. It has been sold lately at 34—up and down sure enough. Two cargoes I under-stand have been purchased, one for the States, the other for Ger-many. Sort-a-sending-coals-to-Newcastle business, tho' in this in-stance I think the coals will pay.

I don't know what to say of yr Fort Vancouver project [unidenti-fied]. I feel sure that if you enter upon it, you will not make anything out of it for 4 or 5 years; that is, sufficient to authorize you in your own mind to think you had enough to go home on. I can only think it is the support of your family that keeps you out here. While you are striving for what you think it necessary to ensure their comfort and happiness, they are deprived of one of the choicest sources of both by your absence. Nearly every letter to me from the girls bears a request (a prayer nearly, so earnest is it) that I would use my influence with you to have you return home. I know, and knew when I left Baltimore, that all your family wished you to return; that Lizzie was fretting herself to death about you. While you were here I did not say all I had heard and seen of Lizzie's grief and unhappiness because I thought you were in a fair way of realizing your wish to make a pile sufficient to satisfy you and I did not think it proper to discourage you, but I cannot see that your Vancouver project will bring you nearer to your object.

The time has passed when men without means can make sudden Fortunes in California. It has suddenly grown into and [page torn] place. Money is here in abundance as ready to [page torn] all channels promising profit as in the old cities [page torn] who win without it must do so by steady perseverance in their beaten track. You are feverish and restless [page torn], very fact of your family depending on your exertions [page torn] for future competency acts as a goading spur to your energies and you are making desparate attempts to gain your point—I think unwisely. You know on what you can depend at home. *I* know they all wish you returned and I think you would best find your comfort and happiness and best compass that of your family by returning. I know what *pride* is, John, that pride which would suffer the rack before yielding and if *I* were *you*, I would not return with nothing in my pocket. But I have no family, no wife weeping for me; no children to ask, where's dad and I might indulge in the luxury of pride, but you, Johnny, have higher claims on you than those of that high strained tyrant. You must not call this advice presumption.

Touching your purchase of stoves from Mssrs. Starr Minstrom & Co., I called there about it and heard from them that they recollected the purchase, had received no letter from you but had a call from a person not long before who had wanted to purchase stoves of them of a certain class, as he had understood they had some of that class of stoves *without hearths*. I am sorry you did not send me the documents, any Bill Lading, Bill act. on Expenses and order to collect as I could doubtless have collected the amount. As it is you had better send me, as near these documents as you can, at once and Write to Mr. Hopkins to send your letter to S[tarr] M.[instrom] & Co. to us, if he has not delivered it.

I have had diarhea for a week. Partners well. Send their respects. Business still dull.

YOURS EVER
Robt. George

* * * * *

Oregon City, April 28 1851

To John Marsh Smith
FRIEND SMITH

I can sell almost all the hams by the lbs at 25 cts. if the[y] are good, so if the[y] can be bought at 15 cts buy them and send them up—that is, keep as many as you think will sell in Portland If you go in jointly and if not tell Mr. Barnhart to sell some of them for me. If you get them send them as soon as you can. I wish you would look out for my canoe along the shore at Portland, and you will much oblige your

FRIEND
H. Burns

* * * * *

Portland, Oregon, May 1851

To Robert George
DEAR BOB

Your favour of Apl 22nd was rec'd a couple of days since. Since my last I cannot report any favourable change in demand or rates of Goods, with a market fully suppl[ied]. There are now lying in this port *Three* Barques and one Schooner, just arrived with full and assorted cargoes direct from the States, and more on the way, and two vessels expected shortly from Canton together with frequent arrivals from San Francisco and generally fair stocks in the hands of merchants, affording sufficiency for the present and prospect of some expected into the future. The accounts from the mines of late have been of rather an encouraging character ... [rest of letter missing].

· · · · ·

Ms Steamer *Northerner*, May 15 1851

To Messrs Corwin Brothers & Co.
Panama
GENTLEMEN

I beg to introduce to you my friend, John Marsh Smith of Baltimore.

Mr. Smith is going home and I give him this letter to use in case of sickness or detention on the Isthmus. And should such a misfortune befall him and he should thereby require funds you may advance him what he needs on his bill on Thomas M. Smith of Baltimore, or on his father-in-law, Mr. Tyson, and I hold myself responsible for the prompt and faithful honor of his drafts.

VERY TRULY YOURS, ETC.
Beverley C. Saunders

· · · · ·

[This letter was presumably forwarded to JMS in Baltimore.]

Baltimore, May 22 1851
[Postmark] Baltimore, May 24, MD

To John Marsh Smith
Care of Cross Hobson & Co.
San Francisco, Cal
DEAR JOHN

It has been a long time since I have written to or rec'd a letter from you, but I have often thought of you and your trials and troubles. My principal object in addressing you at present is to call your attention to an opening which presents itself at this time & leave it for your consideration. I must commence with the melancholy information of the death of James Atkinson. The poor fellow died in New York, where he had gone accompanied by his wife & one child to embark for England. His remains were brought home and intered at Gree[n]mount. Hannah bears her misfortune as well as could be expected. (But to go on), since James death Robert will have to fill his place by someone who can look after the customers of the concern & expresses himself anxious to have you; from what I can learn his views are that if you will come home he will give you one thousand dollars for the first year & proposes if you like the business to advance your interest. Now it does seem to me that the prospect is a fair one, but of course I would not urge you to any measure contrary to your own judgement. It would be pleasant indeed to have you at home once again, & it does seem to me that the present prospect looks fairer than any which is likely to occur.

Sister Lizzie & the little boys spent the day with us yesterday. They were all very well. The boys are fine little fellows. By the way we have lately moved & are living at the corner of St. Paul and Franklin St. All of our mutual friends are quite well. Harriette would be glad to add a P.S. & her love but as I write from the store will hardly have a chance. Since Fred's return he is in business with father & Dungan & though his start is small I consider it better than mine was. Bob is at present in our counting room.

> With much love I remain your
> AFFECTIONATE BROTHER
> James E. Tyson

• • • • •

Oregon City, June 22 1851
[Stamped] Oregon City, Org. June 23

To John Marsh Smith Esq
Baltimore, Maryland
Mr. JM Smith

Dr. Sir I hope you will excuse me for intruding this upon your notice so soon after your arrival among your friends, but believing that in your generous nature you sometimes think of the land you have seen, and the friends you have left behind you, I am induced to believe that a line or two from *Tumwata* would not be unwelcome.[15] As you have some idea of the place I write from, of course you will not expect much news, but if I have not been anticipated I will give you a trial [?] about the election.

I think our friend Thompson of Portland had declared himself a candidate for the legislature before you left. Well, things went on first rate, his right hand Norris was very active for him, so likewise was Barnheart and nearly all the young men in Portland.[16] As the day of election approached excitement began to increase, and there was considerable betting. Thompson you know ran against King.[17] Col. Backinsloch of course was one of Kings champions.[18] Norris and the Col had a bet of some three or four ounces, Barnheart and the Col some two or three moor. May (of the firm of May and Goldsmith) and the Col had a bet of Fifty Dollars.[19] At length the day of election arrived, and the dafter [day after], and Thompson's majorities began to come in from Lynn City & Milton, & King got every vote on Souvies Island,[20] but still Thompson was ahead and there was one or two other precinct to be heard from, but they were Thompson strongholds, and of course would swell his majority, so the opposition gave it up.

Thommsonians were in the best kind of spirits, they nearly worried the Col's life out of him. Capt. Norton, a Kingite, hoisted the flag at half mast, with the Union down.[21] Dryer at the head of a body of Thomsonians went over and remonstrated but the Capt maintained that he would do as he liked with his own property.[22] The Thomsonians then commenced firing Canon, and that brought out the

Canon of the opposition. The poor Siwashes couldn't countenance what the Bostons meant, they thought it a great waste of *polallio*.[23] The Kingites said they would have the last fire, But Thompson heard of it and hired a man to fire all night, so we had a roar of cannon from that evening until the next morning at sunrise, 700 guns in all. In the meantime there was two or three champaighn drinkings at the Col expense. But, lo! on tomorrow, a majority of six came in for *King*. You can imagine what a turn things took after that, better than I can describe it. The flag was run up to the masthead and the Kingites renewed their firing and the poor Thompsonians had to pay for the Champaign & the bets besides. Thompson bore it like a man. I haven't known anything as exciting since I have been in the territory.

The fire company are going to celebrate the 4th. T.G. Dryer is to deliver the oration, then they will proceed to Oregon City on the Willammette. The river is quite high at this time. Any boat can come up here at this time. The bark *Success* is lying here at Allan & McKinleys wharf.[24] The *Lot Whitcomb* has been purchased by the citizens of Oregon City for $50,000 and is undergoing repairs at this place, the little propeller *Blackhawk* brought from San Francisco and owned by Clark, Angel & Hoyt makes daily trips to Portland and back. The *Skukum Chuck* and *Tumwater ain't* no *where* and *I* like Othello find my occupation *gone*.[25] There will soon be three steamboats in opperation above the falls, The Harrises, Lieut Bessells, & Murrys.[26]

Things are going ahead *here awfully*. The news from the mines is pretty good but the Indians are giving the miners some trouble. Gov. Gains has gone out to see what is to be done. Bently has gone to the Umpqua to take a claim.[27] Tom Collins has gone to San Francisco, he expects to get charge of the vessel his brother has. *Old Hugh* has gone to San Francisco, to buy some more sugar I guess. D. Burns & family are all well.[28] I have requested my brother, A.F. Fenwick to call and see you, when he visits Balt. A.[llan] M.[c]K.[inley] & Co. talk of building a store at Canimah and putting me in it.[29] I send you the *Statesman*, with this.[30] I believe I have told you all worth mentioning. Remember me to all of my friends that you may meet up with. I would be glad if you would call on John Murphy, Book Seller on Market Street, you know. Also on Geo. W. Webb-Quiller and remember me to them both.

YOURS IN HASTE

J.A. Sims[31]

I hope you will excuse all mistakes and burn this as soon as you read it.

JAS

• • • • •

Multnomah City, August 3 1851

To John Marsh Smith
in care Cary, Tison & Dungen
Baltimore, Md.
ESTEEMED FRIEND

This day have performed what I should have done long ago, namely fill up a deed for a lot that I promised you when you and myself ware in San Francisco, but you know what a hustle I was in when I came home, But I hope I will not be too late now, and hope you will except as part pay for your kind services tendered to me both here and in California, for which kindness I have not nor will not forget, and now friend Smith if I can do any thing for you here or in San Francisco, name it and I assure you that I will take great pride in doing it.

I was down to San Francisco last June, left on the 21. I will say nothing about fires of that place for you know all about it. I found the business very dull. I bought coffee and shuger, a better article than what I bought last winter, for less mony, but I cannot sell it so that it will pay as much, for this country is almost knee deep with coffee and shuger and good shuger is sold here for six cts per pound and coffee at 14 cts and goods of all kinds in like maner. While I was in California six large vesals came in direct from the states and from China and is selling goods cheeper than I bought mine, so if I get out of this lot of goods with my coat on I will stay out a while.

Capt Beard is here in the *Merchantman*, he leaves in a few days and when he returns he will be marid to the girl he saw at curhs [church]. She and her sister Dr. Barckley's wife and the Docktor and a host of other jentry was at dinner on board the *Merchantman* yesterday.[32] They tuck me along to fill up an odd corner, Well they had a splendid time of it. Ned done his best to make them happy. I forgot to say that a week ago yesterday the Doctor gave a picknick party and Ned was there, and as it was at the spring below my house they stoped in as they were going and invited me to diner. They think a greadle [great deal] of Ned, and the way he loves the *dear* in the Girl is nobody's business.

Barnhart is full partner now and is doing as well as any of them. The Brig. *Amazon* belonging to Winter & Latamer arrived here from China in June with a full cargo,[33] and when the[y] ware in full blast seling, Old Capt Norton came down on the Cargo Brig and all winter was here at the time, so they will have a fine low time of it. Lewis May is winding up in Portland and is going to the States next steamer.

Portland looks sick and I think before the first of Jan next there will be a jenrel smach [smash]. There has been a splendid steam-boat ship[p]et here from the States and put to[ge]ther on the Wil-lamette river above the fall. She is 80 hors power. As to the mines of Oregon, I cannot tell you whether the[y] are good or not because all those from this place returned in a short time, yet old miners comes in with plenty of dust and says they are doing well, so that is the way it gos. But the people of Oregon has no need of going to the mines, they can do better at home, for I do believe the best crops that man has ever seen of all kinds has been Oregon this year.

The emigrants from the States are coming in slowly. I can't tel you anything about the number that will come across the planes this summer, as those that has come in cannot tel how many is behind them, but I think about 1000 wagons—some says two or three [thousand]. My sister and her family from the west is coming, and then all of mine will be her[e] and as soon as I get a little paper in my old pocket for my claim I will go to the lot along side of I sold last year for $400.00 to John Brisbine, he since built a good house on it. It tis a good place for business it being close to the ferry, and I hope some day you will have a fine store on it. I will send you some papers.[34]

My brothers folks are all well. I hope this find you and family well and happy. Write to me if you have time. If I live and be well I hope to be in your city before the first of May next, but during that time I would like to here from you as often as your time will permit.

FROM YOUR FRIEND

H. Burns

•   •   •   •   •

San Francisco, August 30 1851

To John Marsh Smith

DEAR JOHN

I am in receipt of your favor of June 30th, and must say I am very much pleased at your safe arrival home away from friends. You should be a happy dog, With your family centered around you as in days past and no doubt up to this date you are recounting scenes in California & Oregon witnessed by Mr. M. Smith, the veritable John. Well, we certainly have had the devils own luck in this country, but you are among those who really care for your *home.* I [am] still among that class of people so freely called rascals in Balt[imore] with at this present moment about 1 dozen fleas who appear to revel on the fat with which I abound and am so justly proud of. How I write I hardly know, very badly tho, for which please blame the fleas, not me.

Business is most intolerably dull and does not improve in the least I assure you. How the majority of jobless manage to exist is a mystery to me, but with few exceptions nothing has advanced on prices. Segars are bringing about cost, no more. A great number are preparing to leave for home. Bailing & McKee start the steamers, having made a snug fortune each, quick work and easily done, While I have toiled and worked, have been energetic and I hope honest, and am still at the starting point. I have not had one single friend to say one word that would benefit me. But I will leave this subject as I feel passion uncontrollable rise up within me, I wish to get along smoothly and will on to some other topics.

Believe me my dear fellow that I am truly glad to hear of you being among the Drugs & paints and I do hope the tide you have travelled with so long has at last turned flood. I would rather be home working a living than be here doing well, for I swear there is no comfort and no real pleasure. There are some of the best fellows in the world whom I will hate to leave yet there is no place like home, no friend equal a Mother and my mother I do wish to see, God knows how anxious I am to see her kind face again. You say truly my visit will be a satisfaction to my family and friends; to my family no doubt, but where are my friends, save yourself and but few others I have no friends in Balto, that has been proved.

Ned Beard has arrived here but I have not yet seen him. When I told the boys I have received a letter from you they were eager to know the contents, and all desire to be remembered, you have many very warm hearted friends here, and you now are held in good esteem by them.

Spt 1 1851

The *Flying Cloud* arrived yesterday in 89 days from New York, an extraordinary quick run, and which has created some excitment.[35] Since I wrote the previous pages I have seen Ned Beard, he desires to be particularly remembered and told me where his mother was to be found, in Gay St. but I have forgotten the location.

I hope you have been a frequent visitor at Surrey, since your arrival home. If you have not, stand clear of me when I return.

You must excuse this miserable letter, as I am not in writing mood. Write me often. Regards to any *friends* who enquire for me, with best wishes for your future prosperity.

I REMAIN TRULY YR. FRIEND
A.S. Dungan

• • • • •

[The following is all that has survived of a letter—evidently to a newspaper editor—by JMS on his experiences in the West.]

... Contrary to your advice in particular and my friends in general, and pressing invitation from the diggings. To the contrary and not withstanding, "I cut my cords and left all meaner things to low ambition and the pride of Kings." And returned home a busted individual after a two years cruise in an unsuccessful search after the root of all *evil*, which I expected to procure in the same way all other roots are procured by steady application of the Agricultural implement that generally fetches that answer, but having been seduced by the representations of others and an uncontrollable desire to see for myself, I suddenly stopped rooting and went to dam[m]ing. Well, you know, dam[m]ing operation is Speculative and with some People Speculations turns out right and with some its generally over the left. That side I belong to and no doubt as you are a man of experience you can form some idea of the consequences attending such a fate, retrenchment and reform economy. What was economy? going without anything to Eat because I had not the money to pay for it. Editor, when a man gets hungry he reflects and thats the time I begun to think of Oregon, Land that the American Eagle flied over.

I was not long striking the trail and following it up and to my inexpressable joy, found it as I had always heard it represented, a land flowing with Asses Milk and untamed Honey. You may depend upon it, I represent it in its true light, for I know its rich in gold, rich in Timber, its valleys and hills richer, its mountains higher, its cataracts more stupendous, its mill priviledges unequalled, its women Handsomer, its Hogs fatter, its dogs uglier, forming a picture more gigantic than any artists has ever yet been able to execute. But Editor, pressing invitation from these diggings whare I am now located sort of took possession of my senses, and I now left you—feelin[g] bad, sorry to separate myself from so much that I was attached to and feeling worse the further I got from you, but getting company with a fellers Wife and little Ones and some old friends dont only fetch a feller biped to his senses *fast*, but *faster*, and from present prospects I may consider myself fixed and contented. I have detirmined to go with my Brother who is doing a large Drug Business, the firm Smith & Atkinson, the latter a brother in law having died after I left Oregon. I have had various propositions made me since I arrived home, one to return to Oregon, but judging from experience I believe it better for me to remain here where I am well known and with I think a certainty of success....

Notes to Chapter Three

1. Bob George, a family and business friend of JMS; George Gibson, of Lowenstein & Gibson, a general trading company.
2. Degarrs: daguerreotypes.
3. A Baltimore friend of John Curlett, Jr., and JMS and his family.
4. Gold was found in the Klamath Mountains in the southwestern part of what is now Oregon.
5. John P. Gaines was appointed territorial governor of Oregon by President Taylor in 1850, and took office in August in Oregon City, the territorial capital.
6. Orator, statesman and senator from Massachusetts, in 1851 Daniel Webster (1782-1852) was serving as secretary of state under President Fillmore.
7. This is thought to be the daguerreotype from which the frontispiece portrait was painted.
8. Hugh Burns emigrated to Oregon in 1844.
9. Probably the business opened by Henry W. Corbett in March 1851, when he was 24 years old. He rapidly became a prominent citizen of Portland.
10. "Mrs. Captain" was Captain James Hobson's wife, and thus Joseph Hobson's sister-in-law.
11. Burn's land claim, which he called Multnomah City, was across the Willamette River and slightly north of Oregon City.
12. William H. Barnhart was the Portland agent for Wells, Fargo & Company.
13. Chirography: handwriting
14. The rush to the Oregon mines left animals and crops unattended.
15. Chinook for "waterfall," *Tumwata* was a colloquialism for Oregon City, which lies at the falls of the Willamette River.
16. Shubrick Norris was a member of Portland's first City Council, in 1851.
17. R.R. Thompson and William M. King were bitter rivals for a seat in the Territorial Legislature. Thompson, a Democrat, was later an original investor in the Oregon Steam Navigation Co., Oregon's first major business enterprise, and became influential in Portland's business

community. King, a Whig, was backed by the more conservative element, including the *Oregonian*. He, too, became prominent in Portland's development, as the King's Heights section of the city attests.

18. Lt. Col. Jacob B. Backenstos, U.S. Army, was stationed at Oregon City.

19. Lewis May was among the many transient merchants in Oregon City at the time.

20. Lynn City, the present-day West Linn, across the river from Oregon City, was established in 1840 by Robert Moore, Hugh Burn's neighbor to the south; Milton is a small community at the junction of the Willamette and the Columbia; Sauvie Island is a large island in the Columbia.

21. Zachariah C. Norton was master of the *Sequin*, the first ship to sail from San Francisco to Astoria and on to Portland, carrying the mail. He was also a partner in a merchandise and commission business in Portland.

22. Thomas Dryer, the *Oregonian*'s first editor, was a staunch Whig, much in demand as an eloquent speaker.

23. *Siwash*: Chinook jargon for "Indian," here used derogatorily for the Democrats, who were combating the "Bostons," or Whigs; *polallio*: Chinook jargon for "gunpowder."

24. G.T. Allan and A. McKinley owned a general-merchandise, boat-operations and commission business.

25. The *Lot Whitcomb*, named after one of its owners, was the first steamboat built on the Willamette River, at Milwaukie. It was launched on Christmas Day 1850 and competed with the *Columbia*, the only other vessel making the highly profitable run between Portland and Astoria. The small steamer *Black Hawk* was brought to Portland in 1851 from the Sacramento River by its owners, Abernethy, Clarke & Co., for whom it was a money maker. ("Angel," George Abernethy, was a respected Methodist who served as provisional governor from 1845 to 1849, when Oregon became a U.S. territory.) The *SkukumChuck* (Chinook for "rapids") and the *Tumwater* ran between Portland and Oregon City. They were operated by James Colum, who appears to have employed Sims, but evidently competition from the *Black Hawk* was too great for them.

26. The April 4 1851 issue of the *Statesman* notes that "Lieut. Bissell, U.S.N. has arrived to operate a steamer above the falls."

27. The Oregon City *Spectator* had to suspend publication when its printer, S. Bently, left for the mines.

28. Dan Burns was Hugh Burns's brother.

29. Canemah was the loading and unloading point for portage around Willamette Falls.

30. The Oregon City *Statesman* began publication in 1851. Its editor was Asahel Bush, who strongly represented the Democratic viewpoint in the politically charged period as Oregon moved toward statehood, and was known as "the Locofoco editor."

31. Originally from Baltimore, John A. Sims eventually moved to The Dalles, on the Columbia, where he was the Indian agent and representative for Allan, McKinley.
32. Dr. Forbes Barclay appears to have been an employee of the Hudson's Bay Company in 1846. In 1895 he opened a drug store in Oregon City, and later served there as coroner.
33. The *Amazon* is reported to have been the first ship to reach Oregon from China; Gabriel Winter and B.G. Latimer were commission merchants in Oregon City.
34. Although Hugh Burns managed to sell several lots in Multnomah City, the community did not thrive, in large part because of competition from Linn City. In November 1853 most of its buildings were swept away by the high waters of the Willamette River.
35. The *Flying Cloud*, Captain Josiah P. Creesy, master, broke all records when it made the run to San Francisco in 89 days and 21 hours.

CHAPTER FOUR
1852

. . . . .

Multnomah City, February 16 1852

To John Marsh Smith
ESTEEMED FRIEND,

I was at Portland last week and Barnhart gave me a note from you of the 28th of Oct. last which was enclosed in a letter to him, he had it some time before he thought to hand it to me. Their is no person here at present engaged in the Degarratiple [daguerreotype] business, but you may depend that the first opportunity that I have I will send you a view of the places you wish.

I send you enclosed some of those blue beads of diferent Shapes and sizes, and some frequences that the Indians use or did use, so sais tradition, for mony, but now the women use them. Some has them around their nek like beads. Others t[h]rough their nose, across under the nostrils, perhaps you saw some when you were here: also an armaluitt that the women ware on the wrist, all of which I ploughed up today in my field and send them to you just as I found them, for recolect that they ware put there with the owner as all things they possess at there death is put at the place whare they are layed. Where you saw the beads was a large burrying place, I should have said a place of the past, for when I first come to this country I found here in the bushes a hundred canoes with bones, pots pans pi[t]chers, tin kettles and up and all maner of things in and round the canoes, the pots and such thing put on sticks that is stuck in the ground. They punch a hole trough the botom, and also make a large hole in the botom of the canoe. When I was clearing the place I could have got a bucketfull of beads in the canoes.[1]

A shocking accident has hapaned to the propeller *Genrel Warren* near the mouth of Columbia river on Sunday morning Feb 1st, the full account is published in the papers which I will send you. Her cargo was oats, flour & hogs, which if it had arrived in California to meet the present high prices for hogs & oats, Would have sold for at leat $150,000.[2]

This winter is very much the finest that has been since I have come to the country on shore, but up the coast it has been dreadfull, and it is feared that sevearal vesalles bound up from California is lost besides two going down, the schooners *Harriet* and *J.C. Demerest*, Tom Collins master. Capt Jerry Collens left San Francisco Jan 17, has not since been heard of, also Brig *Marshal* and Bark *Success*, and many others.

Ned Beard has been here all winter loading the *Geo & Martha*, he has been laying at the mouth of the Columbia severl weeks waiting to go out, he is to be mari'd on his return. Friend Smith you know the part I took in the matter the first time I saw him. At his earnest request I interaduced the subject to her friends, an act that I have since much regreted, and now a gentleman told Mr. McLoughlin in Presence today that he had a woman on board dresed in men's clothes & calls her Charley. The D. "pitched" right on me and said that me and my Brother interaduced him as a gentleman. Their will be the devil to pay. I expect that Dr. Barckly will be after me about it and how to get out of it I do not know, for if I knew nothing about him I should have said nothing and stand convicted. However I think that their is nothing of it and think Ned will make a good husband, for he is a good hearted young man and stands high here.

MARCH 6 1852. I intended to send th[is] by Dr. Maxwell who left here in the last steam[er] for Washington City but he left a day sooner than I expected. I am going to San Francisco in this steamer that is now due and if I can seen anyone going to Baltimore that I know I will enclose the beads. If not I will send them by the first opportunity. Letter has just come in from Jerry Collens stating that he lost the schooner *Juliet* on the beach about 30 miles south of the Columbia river on the morning of the 28 of January. All hands survived and part of the cargo. She had full loads of merchandise for this country, worth over $60,000. The *John C. Demerest*, Tom Collins master, has not yet be herd of. It is feared that all hands have perished. The other vessels has arrived. The propeller *Seagull* is also lost, no lives, a full cargo for Oregon.[5] Oregon has suffered very much by sea this winter. The *Geo & Martha* has arrive safe in San Francisco, so friend Beard will do well. All the winter that we had has been in the last 8 days, snowing every day, today it rained. Snow all gone and I am glad of on my cows account & hogs.

MARCH 7 1852. The mail from the States has just arrived. Dr. Barkley receive a letter from Mr. Beard. He tells the Dr. that he is out of the *George & Martha* and is coming in a fine ship and will take his little Duck down to San Francisco next time he goes down. He is all right. The Dr. Don't believe a word of it and says it's all false and I am glad, so you may soon expect to here of a big wedding in Oregon City, but I won't be in. I send you five papers. You will find 1 & 4 of a fine wet party. I will send you all of it soon. it tis rich. Names of the acters: Judy Prat, Chickopee Bush, Wick ned M.P. Deady, Arnold Anderson of Astoria, Frank Dr. Wilson, Thotspur Lovejoy, Rex King of log rolers of Portland. The others you don't know.

You shall have it in pam[ph]let form with plates.[4]

FROM YOUR OLD FRIEND AND
WRITE SOON
H. Burns

•   •   •   •   •

To John Marsh Smith
ESTEEMED FRIEND

I received a letter from your kind lady dated July 20 in answer to mine of June 4th in respect to a school for my boy, Which is fully answered in Mrs. Smith's letter, from which I hold myself forever indebted. In a word the promptitude and kindness of your most amiable lady overwhelms me, for full well I know that such real kindness and disinterested friendship is rarely met with, at least by me, and be assured that sch a treasure wont slip through my fingers easily.

I regret to say to you that I don't think it will be in my power to go to the States this fall. When I wrote to you in June last I was in hopes that I could have left before this time, for I thought in three months after I proved up my land claim that it would be allright, but Old man Moore runs his line over mine on the upper end and Mr. Tompkins on the lower, neather [neither] of which can you get one inch of my claim, for I was on mine three months before Moore was on his, and eight years before Tompkins, but the lines has to be settled before we can have our claims surveyed. When that is done then the surveyor gen. will send to Washington the plan for my claim and proof of my settlement and Cultivation, but as soon as the lines is settled and this surveyed then I can go where I please. Their is a greadle of confusion about the lines all over the country, and hundreds will be at Law all their lives. The Oregon Land Law was the worst law that Chongress ever made, all entirely for the benefit of Lawyers.[5]

Capt Norton got judgment against Winton & Colman last June for a large amount. I don't no the amount—all their property in Portland was sold by the sheriff.

Times are very good here now, farmers are in their glory. Wheat at the river at any point that a boat can get to is at $2.50 per bushel, oates [illegible], potatoes $2.00, onions $8.00, butter 50 cts lb, hogs on foot 12 ¢, 19¢ per lb, chickens $1.00 each. Their is also a greadle doing in Lumber business and mony is plenty.

The Emagration to this country this year is larger than any two years heretofore. Their is a greadle of sickness and much sufering among them and half of them not in yet, so reported. We have had many fine rains during the past month which done much good, the whole face of the country looks like spring and the grass is growing fast so that stock will have a good feed all winter, besides the rains has soffined the ground thorough for the farmers to plough and their is more ploughs running now than has been put it all to[ge]-ther for the last four years. Our farmers are wiping the cobwebs from their eyes and some biting their fingers off, because now that all kinds of provisions are high, they have nothing to sell and their mony is getting short. So this year the[y] are determined to have something to sell.

Everything needful will be high here this winter. Their is scarce-ly any coffee or sugar in Oregon at present, nor can it be bought in San Francisco for anything that would justify any person to run the risk of the market. The cargo of the ship [illegible] that reached here six weeks ago from New York has sold at a great profit. Abernathy & Cox had 200 tons on her and Mr. Abernathy told me that he will make more on them than on any other goods he ever bought, the demand is so great.

OCTOBER 3. Richard Lane Esq formerly of the Hudson's Bay Com-pany committed suicide in Oregon City yesterday by cutting his throat. I saw him a few minutes after he don it. It was an awfull gash such as I never saw befor and hope I never will again. He cut the winpipe exce[p]t a small portion at the back part, but cut no blood vessell. He is yet alive 24 hours after. His wife died last year and he has not done well since. He has neglected his business and drank hard. Consequently his business got deranged and some of his creditors here came down on him and he's gave way. I think you must know him as he kept the Hudson Bay Company Store in Ore-gon City when you ware here. He is a small man, and a Gentleman of high respectability.[6]

It tis imosable [impossible] at present for me to tell when I can go to the States. I thought that I could have settled the boundry Lines of my claim last week but the man that run his line over mine on the lower land of my claim has gone to the mines and wont be back until January next. But I may start before that time, if I can I will.

Allow me here to congratulate you on the Birth of a young daugh-ter in your absence and I do hope that this may find the mother and daughter enjoying every happiness that heaven and earth can bestow on them and the same for yourself and all that are yours.[7]

is the sincere wish of your
TRUE FRIEND
H. Burns

Notes to Chapter 4

1. Chinook Indians lived along the banks of the Willamette; Burns's Multnomah City was evidently the site of a burial ground. Still used as trade items in 1850, blue beads were advertised that year in the Sacramento *Placer Times*.
2. An early sidewheeler built in 1844 for the Portland Steam Packet Company in Maine, the *General Warren* was wrecked at Clatsop Beach, south of the Columbia, on January 28 1852, with the loss of 42 lives.
3. The *Juliet* was lost south of Yaquina Bay on the Oregon coast; the *Seagull* on the Humboldt Bar, off the northern California coast, on January 26 1851.
4. The copy of the original pamphlet is in the John Marsh Smith papers of the Oregon Historical Society. The script was written by Breakspear; the characters are thinly disguised members of Oregon's political community, including Asahel Bush, Matthew Deady, Asa Lovejoy, and A.N. King.
5. Land holdings had been in dispute for years. The Donation Land Law of September 1850 granted every male settler over 18 who was a U.S. citizen, or who declared his intention of becoming one by December 1 1851, 320 acres if he were single and 640 acres if he were married within a year of that date. Claims were to be filed with the surveyor general within three months.

   Burns and Moore had long rivaled each other, not only over their land claims, but also over the ferry license and the siting of the provisional government at their respective town sites.
6. A Hudson's Bay clerk in 1837, Richard Lane later assumed ownership of the store in Oregon City. He was also a lawyer, and in 1847 was appointed as judge in Vancouver County. Lane survived his suicide attempt of 1852, and moved first to Olympia and later to The Dalles, where he died in 1877 of an overdose of morphine.
7. Martha Tyson Smith was born on June 28 1852.

CHAPTER FIVE
1853-1857

. . . . .

San Francisco, January 14 1853

To John Marsh Smith
DEAR JOHN

Your favor of Oct 16th, Nov 25th I received by last steamer.

The ship *James Conner* has arrived and was berthed at the wharf yesterday, not yet discharged anything. I note in your instructions relative to the disposal of the goods and will follow them and do all I can to make a good sale. Altho I cannot hold out any expectations of your realizing much of the shipment, I will as you well know do all I can to further your interest.

Burns is in town and doesn't seem to be particularly remembered. He brought the boy down to school and has placed him in the Mission until March when he says he will start for the States. I delivered your messages to him. The old fellow appears to think a great deal of you John and to regret your not becoming an Oregonian.

The two prominent pillars of this glorious Republic that you mention, Sanders & Dungan, expect to be taken down in a few months and I am not disposed to regret it.

You must have a nice time travelling thru Juniper [illegible] & swamps, but you can stand it as you had a glimpse of several Elephants while in this country.

Tom Hamilton has arrived out with his wife and her sister, also Bob Bennett's wife so you see we are obtaining additions to the female society from Balt[imore]. Peter Strobel will leave here on the first in the *Monumental City* for Panama & a market, from thence home. So you will see the lucky gentleman soon.

I have no news. Everything is dull and mud abundant. Long boots outside the pantaloons are the *reigning* fashions. Sacramento City has been burned down and overflown twice.

My regards to all your family, to a good yr my dear fellow and remember me always as your very true friend.

Abe

•   •   •   •   •

Dalles of Columbia, May 28 1853

To John Marsh Smith
MY DEAR FRIEND,

I have no doubt but you have long since forgotten me, but as I have just met with an old Baltimorean on his way home I could not resist the opportunity of intruding myself again on your notice. I have thought perhaps a word or two from an old acquaintance might not prove unacceptable.

There has been quite a number of changes in Oregon since you left us, but I expect some more regular correspondent has kept you pretty well posted; however as news is scarce I will write whatever I may find it convenient without regard to what others may have written. For my part I am the same old *two* and *six* that you left me, and am as anxious to get back to old Maryland as ever. I have been farming ever since you left, but I found it a dull business especially as I had to *batch it*. So I have changed my tactics and am about entering into business at the Dalles with Mssrs. Allan McKinley Co. I am sure I cannot tell you how it is going to pay but at any rate I will hope for the best.

Portland has very much improved and there are some fine houses here now. Some of your old friends still remain, viz Marge, Barnheart, Norris, Robert Thompson, Couch, Flanders, Ogden, etc.[1] Barnheart is doing a fine business and Norris is clerking for him. Thompson is a candidate for the Legislature and I believe the others are all doing well.

Oregon City looks pretty much as it did when you saw it last. There has but a few new houses put up until recently. There are two large wholesale houses being put up there now just above Abernathys. Linn City came very near being washed away last winter, but there is a company putting up some fine mills on that side now. Dr. McLoughlin looks as natural as ever, he made Seventy-five thousand dollars by his mills last winter. Flour was $20 per cwt. Dan Burns and family live at their new place on the hill. Mr. Burns talks sometimes of going to California to live. Mr. Hugh Burns I have understood has gone to the States, if so I suppose you have heard of the death of poor Tom Collins & Ned Beard, both of whom were lost at sea. Gerry Collins is still sailing between Portland and San Francisco.

There is considerable excitement in the Territory now about the election for delegates which is to come off on the sixth of June. Gen. Lane and Judge Skinner are the candidates. I intend to vote for Skinner although I think Lane will be elected, he arrived here with his family about two weeks ago.[2]

Mr. Simpson, the gentleman who will take this to you, came out here last summer across the plains. He has traveled over the greater portion of the Territory and now he is on his way back, he tells me he used to be in the Indian Rubber business on Market St. just below where Fields used to keep. I expect he can tell you a great deal about Oregon, as he seems to be pleased with the country and its future prospects.

How are things progressing in old Baltimore? Have you ever met with any of my old friends and acquaintances? I would be very glad indeed if you would write to me and let me know if you have as many pretty *Pretty Girls in Baltimore* as ever, and if there is any use in *my holding on* until I get back. Girls are getting more plenty in Oregon than they were when you were here, but they cannot compare with what I remember our Maryland girls to be. And as soon as

I make money enough to support myself and some poor *white girl* I am coming back to Baltimore to be a neighbor to you. Should you meet with any of my friends, you will remember me to them. You must answer this scroll and I will continue to let you know how things progress at the Dalles. I must now bid you good bye. Hoping to hear from you soon. I remain Sincerely

YOUR FRIEND,
John A. Sims

• • • • •

[Part of several letters on one][3]

Multnomah, September 6 1857

To John Marsh Smith
FRIEND JOHN

I received a letter from you sometime ago back last April. Well, I kept putting of[f], and from mail to mail until now, waiting to have some news to tel you, & I have not much and that is painful. Dr. John McLoughlin is no more, he died the 3 int at 11 o'clock in the fore noon, and was buried yesterday the 5 in the Catholic Church yard in Oregon City and carid on men shoulders from his house to the grave.

It would be a useless task for me to undertake to tel you that mans worth for I have not the capacity, but the time I hope is not far of when some American historian will do him Justice. I say American *historian* because it is from the American people and the American government that he had received the basest kind of ingratitude—so much that it was the slayer of that Powerful mind and Body such as but few men has ever possessed. And I have no doubt it was this ingratitude from a people whoes government he adopted and loved that shortened his life at least twenty years.[4] Some may say that his mind could not be strong if such things Prayed on it. I say to such that Base ingratitude such [as] fell to his lot has and will destroy the strongest minds that ever has or ever exist. No mor[t]al man can bare up against it, and I firmly believe that it has the distroye[d] him.

Elizabeth Brooke Tyson Smith, 1808-1905, "Dear Lizzie"

Gilbert Tyson Smith (Gilly), 1846-1911, the elder of the "dear little
boys"

Thomas Marsh Smith (Little Tommy), 1848-1908, the younger of the "dear little boys"

Matthew Smith, 1779-1865, and Catherine Marsh
Smith, 1790-1870, parents of John Marsh Smith

Martha Ellicott Tyson, 1795-1873, mother of Elizabeth Brooke Smith

Frederick Tyson, 1828-1901, younger brother of Elizabeth Brooke Smith

Martha Tyson Smith, born in 1852 after
John Marsh Smith returned home

Janie Gambrill Smith, 1864-1954, youngest of the Smith children
and donor of the John Marsh Smith papers to The National Society
of The Colonial Dames of America in the State of Oregon

For the last 15 years I know him well and was much with him. Years past he would speak of the ill treatment he received but would not campain or blame any person, yet I knew full well that it was distroying him, but the last few years at times he would complain of his ill treatment most bitterly. Then I knew the once noble heart was destroyed in the years 42, 43 & 44. That man while at the head of the Hudson Bay Co in this country gave out suptgs [supportings] to the Americans Eimagrants $8500. I mean that amount is yet unpaid and never will for they plead limitation, that they done. The Hudsons Bay Co holds him responsible for it. I come to this country in 42 and I know that if it was not for that man, Dr. McLoughlin, that many that came in the years 42, 43 & 44 that is now welthy and wont pay for the flour that kept them & familys from starving. I say without fear of contradiction that was it not for that man their bones would be bleeching on the banks of the Columbia and Willamette rivers. And how did the[y] pay him? I have told you before, with base ingratitude, so much so that it has caused amany another minded American to bow his head in shame for the shamefull conduct (to say the least) of his countrymen. And what class of the American people has done this? Is it the low elettered [illiterate] not them for most of them has done what all men should do. It is what is wrongly called a better class & many of them preaches of the Gosble of God, that has done it, for it was their vilans [villainous] fallshoods to the government and to Chongress that made that Body take from him his land claim.

On the first of this month old Mr. Moore of the founder of Linn City [West Linn] died. He was older than Dr. McLoughlin, he being 75 yrs old & Mr. Moore 80 yrs old. Did you [know] Mr. Moore when here, he owned the claim above mine on the river and came one year before me.

I have but little news to tel you. The convention to form a State Constitution is now in session at Salem, so that we may become a state this winter and yet. not withstanding the constitution, I think will be a good one yet it will be voated down by the people for the black republickens is moving heaven & [e]arth to stave it of[f]m not withstanding they hav their regular ticket at the election.[5]

What has become of Jim Lea, has he gone home? When he left

here he promised to do some business for me in San Francisco, but I have never heard of him since he left here.

We are all well and hope this finds you & family the same, my wished to all your friends, wricht soon.

YOUR FRIEND

H Burns

Notes to Chapter Five

1. Captain John H. Couch, of Newburyport, Massachusetts, made his first trip to the Oregon Country in 1839, sailing the brig *Maryland* around Cape Horn. He left after establishing a claim in 1845 at the site of present-day Portland, and returned in 1849 with his brother-in-law, George H. Flanders, in their bark *Madonna* with a shipload of goods for sale. Couch became a merchant and banker, and Flanders established a San Francisco-Portland run on the *Madonna.*

2. General Joseph Lane, a southerner and a staunch Democrat, was appointed the first territorial governor by President Polk, a position he held from March 1849 to June 1850, when he was replaced by Gaines (see Note 5, 1851). Judge Alonzo A. Skinner, a Whig, had been appointed circuit judge by Governor Abernethy, and served as Indian agent in the Rogue River area.

3. Several typed copies of letters from Hugh Burns to JMS, but not the handwritten originals, are in the John Marsh Smith collection. Dated from May 1853 to February 1856, they are mainly about Burns's own affairs, and have not been included in this publication. Some are devoted to his concern for a family down on its luck, to his provisions for the education of two orphaned nieces, and to his arrangements for deeding a section of Multnomah City to JMS. Burns took the papers for this transaction (now in the collection) "to the states," when he went east in May 1853. He also took more trade beads to give Martha Ellicott Tyson, to whom he eventually sent a quiver and arrows.

4. Although McLoughlin became an American citizen in 1851, having initiated steps to do so in 1845, he was not permitted to keep the lands he had acquired.

5. The issue of slavery was a bitter one as Oregon moved toward statehood. The Democratic candidate, Lane, was careful to avoid commitment on the subject. Skinner's Whig party had splintered over the slavery issue. The anti-slavery group evolved into the Republican Party and was known as "the black republicans."

SOURCES

Bancroft, Hubert Howe, *The History of California*, Vol. 6 (1848-1859), San Francisco, The History Company, 1888.

———, *The History of Oregon*, Vol. 2 (1848-1888), San Francisco, The History Company, 1888.

Bean, Walton, *California, an Interpretive History*, New York, McGraw-Hill, 1968.

Brooks, Howard C. and Ramp, Lan, *Gold and Silver in Oregon*, Portland, Durham and Downey, 1968.

Carey, Charles H., LLD., *A General History of Oregon*, Portland, Metropolitan Press, 1936.

Churchill, Charles W., *Fortunes Are for the Few*, edited by Duane Smith and David T. Weber, San Diego, San Diego Historical Society, 1977.

Clark, Arthur H., *The Clipper Ship Era, 1843-1869*, New York and London, G.P. Putnam's Sons, 1910.

Corning, Howard McKinley, *Willamette Landings, Ghost Towns of the River*, Portland, Oregon Historical Society, 1973.

Cross, Ralph Herbert, *Early Inns of California, 1844-1869*, San Francisco, Cross and Brandt, 1954.

Cutler, Carl C., *Greyhounds of the Sea, the Story of the American Clipper Ship*, Annapolis, U.S. Naval Institute, 1930.

Darbee, Herbert C., *A Glossary of Old Lamps and Lighting Devices*, Nashville, American Association for State and Local History technical leaflet No. 30, 2nd rev. ed., Nashville, *History News 20*, no. 8, 1976.

Frickstad, Walter N., *A Century of California Post Offices*, Oakland, Oakland Philatelic Society, 1955.

Gaston, Joseph, *Portland, Oregon, Its History and Its Builders*, Chicago-Portland, The S.J. Clarke Publishing Co., 1911.

Gibbons, Boyd, "The Itch to Move West," *National Geographic*, August 1986, p. 154.

Gibbs, James A., *Shipwrecks of the Pacific Coast*, Portland, Binfords and Mort, 1957.

———, *Pacific Graveyard, A Narrative of Shipwrecks Where the Columbia Meets the Pacific Ocean*, Portland, Binfords and Mort, 1964.

Holliday, J.S., *The World Rushed In*, New York, Simon and Schuster, 1981.

Johansen, Dorothy O., and Gates, Charles M., *Empire of the Columbia, A History of the Pacific Northwest*, New York, Harper and Row, 1967.

Kemble, John H., *The Panama Route, 1848-1869*, Berkeley, University of California Press, 1943.

Krutch, Joseph Wood, *Herbal*, New York, G.P. Putnam's Sons, 1965.

Lewis, Oscar, *Sea Routes to the Gold Fields: The Migration by Water to California in 1849-1852*, New York, Alfred Knopf, 1949.

Little, William E., and Weiss, James E., eds., *Blacks in Oregon*, Portland, Black Studies Center and the Center for Population Research and Census, Portland State University, 1978.

Long, Frederick J., *Dictionary of the Chinook Jargon*, Seattle, Lowman and Hanford Co., 1909.

McArthur, Lewis A., *Oregon Geographic Names*, Portland, Western Imprints, The Press of the Oregon Historical Society, 1982.

McLagan, Elizabeth, *A Peculiar Paradise, a History of Blacks in Oregon, 1788-1940*, Portland, The Georgian Press, 1980.

Paul, Rodman W., *The California Gold Discovery: Sources, Documents, Accounts and Memoirs Relating to the Discovery of Gold at Sutter's Mill*, Georgetown, The Talisman Press, 1966.

Sacramento Placer Times, Sacramento, April 1849-July 1850.

Shinn, Charles Howard, *Mining Camps: A Study in American Frontier Government*, New York, Alfred Knopf, 1947.

The Spectator, Oregon City, 1849-1857.

The Statesman, Oregon City, 1851-1853.

Stillman, J.D.B., *The Gold Rush Letters of J.D.B. Stillman*, Palo Alto, Lewis Osborn, 1967.

The Sun, Baltimore, January 22 1905.

Taylor, Bayard, *Eldorado or Adventures in the Path of Empire: Comprising a Voyage to California via Panama, Life in San Francisco and Monterey, Pictures of the Gold Region, and Experiences of Mexican Travel*, New York, G.P. Putnam, 1864.

Throckmorton, Arthur L., *Oregon Argonauts*, Portland, Oregon Historical Society, 1961.

U.S. Federal Writers' Project of the Works Progress Administration for the City of New Orleans, *New Orleans City Guide*, Boston, Houghton Mifflin Co., 1938.

FAMILY TREE

Matthew Smith
1779-1865
married
August 23, 1809
Catharine Marsh
1790-1870

- Thomas Marsh Smith (The Elder)
  born August 6, 181_
- JOHN MARSH SMITH
  born August 20, 1818
- Hannah Ann Smith
  born April 26, 1821
- Mary Marsh Smith
  born October 14, 1823
- Anthony Marsh Smith (Tony)
  born May 29, 1826
- Sara R. Smith (*married Robert Tyson*)
  born April 5, 1830
- Catherine Ellen Smith
  born September 14, 1831
- Matthew Marsh Smith
  born January 21, 1834

Nathan Tyson
1787-1867
married
September 27, 1815
Martha Ellicott
1795-1873

- James Tyson
  born August 21, 1816
- ELIZABETH BROOKE TYSON
  born March 3, 1818
- Henry Tyson
  born November 18, 1820
- Isabelle Tyson (Belle)
  born March 17, 1823
- Anne Tyson
  born February 26, 1825
- FREDERICK TYSON
  born April 17, 1828
- Robert Tyson (*married Sarah R. Smith*)
  born March 25, 1830
- Lucy Tyson
  born March 20, 1833

John Marsh Smith
1818-1890
married
May 23, 1843
Elizabeth Brooke Tyson
1818-1905

- Gilbert Tyson Smith (Gilly)
  born April 30, 1846
- Thomas Marsh Smith (Little Tommy)
  born January 28, 1848
- Martha Tyson Smith
  born June 28, 1852
- Janie Gambrill Smith
  born March 8, 1864
  (*donated papers making this book possible*)

Martha Tyson Smith
1852-n.d.
married
April 11, 1877
Samuel Hopkins
n.d.

- Samuel H. Hopkins
  born June 7, 1878
- Matthew S. Hopkins
  born December 30, 1879
- Elizabeth Schofield Brooke Hopkins
  born December 8, 1882
- Mary Randolph Hopkins
  born December 1, 1888
- Alda Tyson Hopkins
  born March 13, 1891

Alda Tyson Hopkins
1891-1969
married
n.d.
James Clark
n.d.

- JOHN L. CLARK
  born December 15, 1914
- James Clark, Jr.
  born December 19, 1918
- Joseph Hopkins Clark
  n.d.

APPENDIX

Excerpts from

ELDORADO

or

Adventures in the Path of Empire:

comprising

A Voyage to California, via Panama;

Life in San Francisco and Monterey;

Pictures of the Gold Region,

and

Experiences of Mexican Travel.

by
Bayard Taylor

Chapter I: From New York to Chagres

On the 28th of June, 1849, I sailed from New York, in the U.S. Mail steamship *Falcon*, bound for Chagres....

After doubling Cape Hatteras, on the second day out, our monotonous life was varied by the discovery of a distant wreck, Captain Hartstein instantly turned the *Falcon*'s head towards her, and after an hour's run we came up with her. The sea for some distance around was strewed with barrels, fragments of bulwarks, stanchions and broken spars. She was a schooner of a hundred tons, lying on her beam ends and water-logged. Her mainmast was gone, the foremast broken at the yard and the bowsprit snapped off and lying across her bows. The mass of spars and rigging drifted by her side, surging drearily on the heavy sea. Not a soul was aboard, and we made many conjectures as to their fate....

[After lying of Charleston and Havana, the *Falcon* reached New Orleans.]

I found New Orleans remarkably dull and healthy. The city was enjoying an interregnum between the departure of the cholera and the arrival of the yellow fever....

The *Falcon* was detained four days, which severely tested the temper of my impatient shipmates.... The hour of departure at length arrived.... Our deck became populous with tall, gaunt Mississipians and Arkansans, Missouri squatters who had pulled up their stakes yet another time, and an ominous number of professed gamblers. All were going to seek their fortunes in California, but very few had an definite idea of the country or the voyage to be made before reaching it. There were among them some new varieties of the American—long, loosely-jointed men, with large hands and feet and limbs which would still be awkward, whatever the fashion of their clothes. Their faces were lengthened, deeply sallow, overhung by straggling locks of straight black hair, and wore an expression of settled melancholy. The corners of their mouths curved downwards, the upper lip drawn slightly over the under one, giving to the lower part of the face that cast of destructiveness peculiar to the Indian. These men chewed tobacco at a ruinous rate, and spent their time either in dozing at full length on the deck or going into the fore-cabin for 'drinks.' Each one of them carried arms enough for a small company and breathed defiance to all foreigners.

We had a voyage of seven days, devoid of incident, to the Isthmus....

Chagres lies about eight miles to the west of this bay, but the mouth of the river is so narrow that the place is not seen till you run close upon it. The eastern shore is high and steep, cloven with ravines which roll their floods of tropical vegetation down to the sea. The old castle of San Lorenzo crowns the point, occupying a position somewhat similar to the Moro Castle at Havana, and equally impregnable....

We came to anchor about half past four. The deck was already covered with luggage and everybody was anxious to leave first. Our captain, clerk, and a bearer of dispatches, were pulled ashore in the steamer's boat.... The clerk, on his return, ... told us that the Pa-

cific steamer would sail from Panama on the 1st of August, and ...
the only canoes to be had that night were already taken.... We resigned ourselves to another night on board, with a bare chance of
sleep in the disordered state-rooms and among the piles of luggage....

Chapter II: Crossing the Isthmus

I left the *Falcon* at day-break in the ship's boat.... Piling up our
luggage on the shore, each one set about seaching for the canoes
which had been engaged the night previous, but, without a single
exception, the natives were not to be found, or when found, had
broken their bargains. Everybody ran hither and thither in great
excitment, anxious to be off before everybody else, and hurrying
the naked boatmen, all to no purpose. The canoes were beached on
the mud, and their owners engaged in re-thatching their covers
with split leaves of the palm. The doors of the huts were filled with
men and women, each in a single cotton garment, composedly
smoking their cigars, while numbers of children, in Nature's own
clothing, tumbled about in the sun. Having started without breakfast, I went to the "Crescent City" Hotel, a hut with a floor to it, but
could get nothing. Some of my friends had fared better at one of the
native huts, and I sat down to the remains of their meal, which was
spread on a hen-coop beside the door....

A returning Californian had just reached the place, with a box
containing $22,000 in gold-dust, and a four-pound lump in one
hand. The impatience and excitement of the passengers, already at
a high pitch, was greatly increased by his appearance. Life and
death were small matters compared with immediate departure
from Chagres.... The boatmen, knowing very well that two more
steamers were due the next day, remained provokingly cool and
unconcerned. They had not seen six months of emigration without
learning something of the American habit of going at full speed.
The word of starting in use on the Chagres River, is "go-ahead!"
Captain C____ and Mr. M____, of Baltimore, and myself, were
obliged to pay $15 each, for a canoe to Cruces.... Our luggage was
stowed away, we took our seats and raised our umbrellas, but the

men had gone off for provisions and were not to be found. All the other canoes were equally in limbo. The sun blazed down on the swampy shores, and visions of yellow fever came into the minds of the more timid travelers.... Our own men appeared towards noon, with a bag of rice and dried pork, and an armful of sugar-cane. A few strokes of their broad paddles took us from the excitement and noise of the landing-place to the seclusion and beauty of the river scenery....

... There is nothing in the world comparable to these forests. No description that I have ever read conveys an idea of the splendid overplus of vegetable life within the tropics....

In the afternoon we reached Gatun, a small village of bamboo huts, thatched with palm-leaves, on the right bank of the river. The canoes which preceded us had already stopped, and the boatmen, who have a mutual understanding, had decided to remain all night.... Two wooden drums, beaten by boys, in another part of the village, gave signs of a coming fandango, and as it was Sunday night, all the natives were out in their best dresses. They are a very cleanly people, bathing daily, and changing their dresses as often as they are soiled. The children have their heads shaved from the crown to the neck and as they go about naked, with abdomens unnaturally distended, from an exclusive vegetable diet, are odd figures enough. They have bright black eyes, and are quick and intelligent in their speech and motions.

The inside of our hut was but a single room, in which all the household operations were carried on. A notched pole, serving as a ladder, led to a sleeping loft, under the pyramidal roof of thatch. Here a number of the emigrants who arrived late were stowed away on a rattling floor of cane, covered with hides. After a supper of pork and coffee, I made my day's notes by the light of a miserable starveling candle, stuck in an empty bottle, but had not written far before my paper was covered with fleas. The owner of the hut swung my hammock meanwhile, and I turned in to secure it for the night. To lie there was one thing, to sleep another. A dozen natives crowded round the table, drinking their aguardiente and disputing vehemently; the cooking fire was on one side of me, and everyone that passed to and fro was sure to give me a thump, while my weight swung the hammock so low, that all the dogs on the premises were constantly rubbing their backs under me. I was just sinking into a doze, when my head was so violently agitated that I started up in some alarm. It was but a quarrel about payment between the Señora and a boatman, one standing on either side. From their angry gestures, my own head and not the reckoning, seemed the subject of contention.

Our men were to have started at midnight, but it was two hours later before we could rouse and muster them together. We went silently and rapidly up the river till sunrise, when we reached a cluster of huts called Dos Hermanos (Two Brothers.) . . . By the time we had gained the ranche of Palo Matida a sudden cold wind came over the forests, and the air was at once darkened. We sprang ashore and barely reached the hut . . . when the rain broke over us, as if the sky had caved in. A dozen lines of white electric heat ran down from the zenith, followed by crashes of thunder, which I could feel throbbing in the earth under my feet. The rain drove into one side of the cabin and out the other, but we wrapped ourselves in India-rubber cloth and kept out the wet and chilling air. During the whole day the river rose rapidly and we were obliged to hug the bank closely, running under the boughs of trees and drawing ourselves up the rapids by those that hung low.

I crept out of the snug nest where we were all stowed as closely as three unfledged sparrows, and took my seat between Juan and Ambrosio, protected from the rain by an India-rubber poncho. The clothing of our men was likewise waterproof, but without seam or fold. It gave no hindrance to the free play of their muscles, as they deftly and rapidly plied the broad paddles.

. . . We stopped the second night at Peña Blanca, (the White Rock), where I slept in the loft of a hut, on the floor, in the midst of the family and six other travelers. We started at sunrise, hoping to reach Gorgona the same night, but ran upon a sunken log and were detained some time. . . .

The character of the scenery changed somewhat as we advanced. The air was purer, and the banks more bold and steep. The country showed more signs of cultivation, and in many places the forest had been lopped away to make room for fields of maize, plantain and rice. But the vegetation was still that of the tropics and many were the long and lonely reaches of the river, where we glided between piled masses of bloom and greenery....

We stopped four hours short of Gorgona, at the hacienda of San Pablo, the residence of Padre Dutaris, curé of all the interior.... I slept soundly ... and only awoke at four o'clock next morning, to hurry our men in leaving for Gorgona.

As we neared Gorgona, our men began repeating the ominous words: "Cruces—mucha colera." We had, in fact, already heard of the prevalence of cholera there, but doubted, none the less, their wish to shorten the journey. On climbing the bank to the village, I called immediately at the store of Mr. Miller, the only American resident, who informed me that several passengers by the *Falcon* had already left for Panama, the route being reported passable. In the door of the alcalde's house, near at hand, I met Mr. Powers, who had left New York a short time previous to my departure, and was about starting for Panama on foot, mules being very scarce.... [However, Taylor and his companions were able to obtain horses.] Next morning at daybreak ... we started off with a guide, trusting our baggage to the honesty of our host [the Alcalde of Gorgona], who promised to send it the same day. The path at the outset was bad enough, but as the wood grew deeper and darker and the tough clay soil held the rains which had fallen, it became finally a narrow gully, filled with mud nearly to our horses' bellies. Descending the steep sides of the hills, they would step or slide down almost precipitous passes, bringing up all straight at the bottom, and climbing the opposite sides like cats. So strong is their mutual confidence that they invariably step in each other's tracks, and a great part of the road is thus worn into holes three feet deep and filled with water and soft mud, which spirts upward as they go, coating the rider from head to foot.

The mountain range in the interior is broken and irregular. The road passes over the lower ridges and projecting spurs of the main chain, covered nearly the whole distance to Panama by dense forests. Above us spread a roof of transparent green, through which few rays of the sunlight fell. The only sounds in that leafy wilderness were the chattering of monkeys as they cracked the palm-nuts, and the scream of parrots, flying from tree to tree. In the deepest ravines spent mules frequently lay dead, and high above them, on the large boughs, the bald vultures waited silently for us to pass. We overtook many trains of luggage, packed on the backs of bulls and horses, tied head-to-tail in long files. At intervals on the road, we saw a solitary ranche, with a cleared space about it, but all the natives could furnish us was a cup of thick, black coffee.

After ascending for a considerable distance, in the first half of our journey, we came to a level table-land, covered with palms, with a higher ridge beyond it. Our horses climbed it with some labor, went down the other side through clefts and gullies which seemed impassable, and brought us to a stream of milky blue water, which, on ascertaining its course with a compass, I found to be a tributary of the Rio Grande, flowing into the Pacific at Panama. We now hoped the worst part of our route was over, but this was a terrible deception. Scrambling up ravines of slippery clay, we went for miles through swamps and thickets, urging forward our jaded beasts by shouting and beating. Going down a precipitous bank, washed soft by the rains, my horse slipped and made a descent of ten feet, landing on one bank and I on another. He rose quietly, disengaged his head from the mud and stood, flank-deep, waiting till I stepped across his back and went forward, my legs lifted to his neck. This same adventure happened several times to each of us on the passage across ... we finally struck the remains of the paved road constructed by the buccaneers when they held Panama. I now looked eagerly forward for the Pacific, but every ridge showed another in advance, and it grew dark with a rain coming up. At last [our guide] put on a pair of pantaloons. This was a welcome sign to us, and in fact, we soon after smelt the salt air of the Pacific, and could distinguish huts on either side of the road. These gave place to stone houses and massive ruined edifices, overgrown with vegetation. We passed a plaza and magnificent church, rode down an open space fronting the bay, under a heavy gate-way, across another plaza and through two or three narrow streets, hailed by Americans all the way with: "Are you the *Falcon*'s passengers?" "From Gorgona?" "From Cruces?" till our guide brought us up at the Hotel Americano.

Thus terminated my five days' journey across the Isthmus—decidedly more novel, grotesque and adventurous than any trip of similar length in the world.

Chapter III: Scenes in Panama

Some of the passengers ... were obliged to remain in Panama another month, since their luggage did not arrive before the sailing of the steamer.

The next day nearly all of our passengers came in. . . . There had been a heavy rain during the night, and the Gorgona road, already next to impassable, became actually perilous. . . .

The roads from Cruces and Gorgona enter on the eastern side of the city, as well as the line of the railroad survey. The latter, after leaving Limon Bay, runs on the north side of the Chagres River till it reaches Gorgona, continuing thence to Panama in the same general course as the mule route. It will probably be extended down the Bay to some point opposite the island of Taboga, which is marked out by Nature as the future anchorage ground and dépôt of all the lines touching at Panama. The engineers of the survey accomplished a great work in fixing the route within so short a space of time. . . .

Panama is one of the most picturesque cities on the American Continent. . . . There is one angle of the walls where you can look out of a cracked watchtower on the sparkling swells of the Pacific, ridden by flocks of snow-white pelicans and the rolling canoes of the natives—where your vision, following the entire curve of the Gulf, takes in on either side nearly a hundred miles of shore. . . .

There were about seven hundred emigrants waiting for passage, when I reached Panama. All the tickets the steamer could possibly receive had been issued and so great was the anxiety to get on, that double price, $600, was frequently paid for a ticket to San Francisco. A few days before we came, there was a most violent excitement on the subject, and as the only way to terminate the dispute, it was finally agreed to dispose by lot of all the tickets for sale. The emigrants were all numbered, and those with tickets for sailing vessels or other steamers excluded. The remainder then drew, there being fifty-two tickets to near three hundred passengers. This quieted the excitement for the time, though there was still a continual under-current of speculation and intrigue which was curious to observe. The disappointed candidates, for the most part took passage in sailing vessels, with a prospect of seventy days' voyage before them.... I was well satisfied to leave Panama at the time; the cholera, which had already carried off one-fourth of the native population, was making havoc among the Americans, and several of the *Falcon*'s passengers lay at the point of death.

Chapter IV: The Pacific Coast of Mexico

... A voyage from Panama to San Francisco in the year 1849, can hardly be compared to sea-life in any other part of the world or at any previous period. Our vessel was crowded fore and aft: exercise was rendered quite impossible and sleep was each night a new experiment, for the success of which we were truly grateful.... Coffee was served in the cabin; but, as many of the passengers imagined that, because they had paid a high price for their tickets, they were conscientiously obligated to drink three cups, the late-comers got a very scanty allowance. The breakfast hour was nine, and the table was obliged to be fully set twice. At the first tingle of the bell, all hands started as if a shot had exploded among them; conversation was broken off in the middle of a word; the deck was instantly cleared, and the passengers, tumbling pell-mell down the cabin-stairs, found every seat taken by others who had probably been sitting in them for half an hour....

Among our company of two hundred and fifty, there were, of course, many gentlemen of marked refinement and intelligence from various parts of the Union—enough, probably, to leaven the large lump of selfishness and blackguardism into which we were thrown. I believe the controlling portion of the California emigration is intelligent, orderly and peaceable; yet I never witnessed so many disgusting exhibitions of the lowest passions of humanity, as during the voyage. At sea or among the mountains, men completely lose the little arts of dissimulation they practise in society....

The heat, during this part of the voyage was intolerable. The thermometer ranged from 82° to 84° at night, and 86° to 90° by day— a lower temperature than we frequently feel in the North, but attended by an enervating languor such as I have never before experienced.

After a week of this kind of existence we passed the sun's latitude, and made the mountains of Mexico. The next night we came-to at the entrance of the harbor of Acapulco, while the ship's boat went to the city, some two miles distant. . . .

On the third morning from Acapulco, we saw the lofty group of mountains bounding the roadstead of San Blas on the East. The islands called Las Tres Marias were visible, ten miles distant, on our left. . . . [At San Blas we] were soon . . . visited by the Alcalde, who after exchanging the ordinary courtesies informed us there were plenty of provisions on shore, and departed, saying nothing of quarantine. . . . We landed on a beach, ancle-deep in sand and covered with mustangs, mules and donkeys, with a sprinkling of natives. Our passengers were busy all over the village, lugging strings of bananas and plantains, buying cool water-jars of porous earth, gathering limes and oranges from the trees, or regaling themselves at the fondas with fresh spring-water, (not always unmixed,) tortillas and fried pork. . . .

In company with some friends, I set out for the old Presidio on the cliff. The road led through swampy forests till we reached the foot of the ascent. . . . Up we went, scrambling over loose stones, between banana thickets and flowering shrubs, till we gained a rocky spur near the summit. Here the view to the north, toward Mazatlan, was very fine. Across the marshy plain many leagues in breadth, bordering the sea, we traced the Rio Grande of the West by the groves of sycamore on its banks; beyond it another lateral chain of the Sierra Madre rose to the clouds. Turning again, we entered a deserted court-yard, fronted by the fort, which had a covered gallery on the inside. The walls were broken down, the deep wells in the rock choked up and the stone pillars and gateways overrun with rank vines. From the parapet, the whole roadstead of San Blas lay at our feet, and our steamer, two miles off, seemed to be within hail.

This plaza opened on another and larger one, completely covered with tall weeds, among which the native pigs rooted and meditated by turns. A fine old church, at the farther end, was going to ruin, and the useless bells still hung in its towers. Some of the houses were inhabited, and we procured from the natives fresh water and delicious bananas. The aspect of the whole place, picturesque in its desolation, impressed me more than anything on the journey, except the church of San Felipe, at Panama.

... Few ports present a more picturesque appearance from the sea than Mazatlan. The harbor, or roadstead, open on the west to the unbroken swells of the Pacific, is protected on the north and south by what were once mountain promontories, now split into parallel chains of islands, separated by narrow channels of sea. Their sides are scarred with crags, terminating toward the sea in precipices of dark red rock, with deep caverns at the base, into which the surf continually dashes. On approaching the road, these islands open one beyond the other, like a succession of shifting views, the last revealing the white walls of Mazatlan, rising gradually from the water, with a beautiful back-ground of dim blue mountains. The sky was of a dazzling purity, and the whole scene had that same clearness of outline and enchanting harmony of color which give the landscapes of Italy their greatest charm. As we ran westward on the Tropic of Cancer across the mouth of the Gulf, nothing could exceed the purity of the atmosphere.

Chapter V: The Coast of California

"There is California!" was the cry next morning at sunrise. "Where?" "Off the starboard bow." I rose on my bunk in one of the deck state-rooms, and looking out of the window, watched the purple mountains of the Peninsula, as they rose in the fresh, inspiring air. We were opposite its southern extremity, and I scanned the brown and sterile coast with a glass, searching for anything like vegetation. The whole country appeared to be a mass of nearly naked rock, nourishing only a few cacti and some stunted shrubs. At the extreme end of the Peninsula the valley of San José opens inland between two ranges of lofty granite mountains. Its beautiful green level, several miles in width, stretched back as far as the eye could reach.... The scenery around it corresponded strikingly with descriptions of Syria and Palestine. The bare, yellow crags glowed in the sun with dazzling intensity, and a chain of splintered peaks in the distance wore the softest shade of violet. In spite of the forbidding appearance of the coast, a more peculiar and interesting picture than it gave can hardly be found on the Pacific. Cape San Lucas, which we passed toward evening, is a bold bluff of native granite, broken into isolated rocks at its points, which present the appearance of three distinct and perfectly-formed pyramids. The white, glistening rock is pierced at its base by hollow caverns and arches, some of which are fifteen or twenty feet high, giving glimpses of the ocean beyond....

Two mornings after [the 12th of August], I saw the sun rise behind the mountains back of San Diego. Point Loma, at the extremity of the bay, came in sight on the left and in less than an hour we were at anchor before the hide-houses at the landing place. The southern shore of the bay is low and sandy; from the bluff hights on the opposite side a narrow strip of shingly beach makes out into the sea, like a natural breakwater, leaving an entrance not more than three hundred yards broad. The harbor is the finest on the Pacific, with the exception of Acapulco, and capable of easy and complete defense. The old hide-houses are built at the foot of the hills just inside the bay, and a fine road along the shore leads to the town of San Diego, which is situated on a plain, three miles distant and barely visible from the anchorage. Above the houses, on a little eminence, several tents were planted, and a short distance further were several recent graves, surrounding by paling. A number of people were clustered on the beach, and boats laden with passengers and freight, instantly put off to us. In a few minutes after our gun was fired, we could see horsemen coming down from San Diego at full gallop, one of whom carried behind him a lady in graceful riding costume. In the first boat were Colonel Weller, U.S. Boundary Commissioner, and Major Hill, of the Army. Then followed a number of men, lank and brown "as is the ribbed sea-sand"—men with long hair and beards, and faces from which the rigid expression of suffering was scarcely relaxed. They were the first of the overland emigrants by the Gila route, who had reached San Diego a few days before. Their clothes were in tatters, their boots, in many cases, replaced by moccasins, and, except their rifles and some small packages rolled in deerskin, they had nothing left of the abundant stores with which they left home.

We hove anchor in half an hour, and again rounded Point Loma, our number increased by more than fifty passengers.... Taking them as the average experience of the thirty thousand emigrants who last year crossed the Plains, this California Crusade will more than equal the great military expeditions of the Middle Ages in magnitude, peril and adventure. The amount of suffering which must have been endured in the savage mountain passes and herbless deserts of the interior, cannot be told in words....

At last the voyage is drawing to a close. Fifty-one days have elapsed since leaving New York, in which time we have, in a manner, coasted both sides of the North-American Continent, from the parallel of 40°N. to its termination, within a few degrees of the Equator, over seas once ploughed by the keels of Columbus and Balboa, of Grijalva and Sebastian Viscain. All is excitement on board; the Captain has just taken his noon observation. We are running along the shore, within six or eight miles' distance; the hills are bare and sandy, but loom up finely through the deep blue haze....

An hour later; we are in front of the entrance to San Francisco Bay. The mountains on the northern side are 3,000 feet in hight, and come boldly down to the sea. As the view opens through the splendid strait, three or four miles in width, the island rock of Alcatraz appears, gleaming white in the distance. An inward-bound ship follows close on our wake, urged on by wind and tide. There is a small fort perched among the trees on our right, where the strait is narrowest, and a glance at the formation of the hills shows that this pass might be made impregnable as Gibraltar. The town is still concealed behind the promontory around which the Bay turns to the southward, but between Alcatraz and the island of Yerba Buena, now coming into sight, I can see vessels at anchor. High through the vapor in front, and thirty miles distant, rises the peak of Monte Diablo, which overlooks everything between the Sierra Nevada and the Ocean. On our left opens the bight of Sousolito, where the U.S. propeller *Massachusetts* and several other vessels are at anchor.

At last we are through the Golden Gate—fit name for such a magnificent portal to the commerce of the Pacific! Yerba Buena Island is in front; southward and westward opens the renowned harbor, crowded with the shipping of the world, mast behind mast and vessel behind vessel, the flags of all nations fluttering in the breeze! Around the curving shore of the Bay and upon the sides of three hills which rise steeply from the water, the middle one receding so as to form a bold amphitheatre, the town is planted and seems scarcely yet to have taken root, for tents, canvas, plank, mud and adobe houses are mingled together with the least apparent attempt at order and durability. But I am not yet on shore. The gun of the *Panama* has just announced our arrival to the people on land. We glide on with the tide, past the U.S. ship *Ohio* and opposite the main landing, outside of the forest of masts. A dozen boats are creeping out to us over the water; the signal is given—the anchor drops—our voyage is over.

INDEX

Abernethy & Cox, 159, 163

Abernethy, Governor George, 152, 159, 166 n

Acapulco, 21, 24, 184

Adams Express, 40

Adams, H. Q., 134, 136

Allen, G. T., 152 n

Allen, R. T. P., 52

Allan & McKinley, 145, 152 n, 162

Amazon, 147, 153 n

American River, 49, 119 n

American River, Middle Fork, 54, 65, 72, 82, 97

American River, North Fork, 54, 72, 97

Astoria, 2, 112, 114, 116, 121 n, 123, 128, 129, 130, 152 n

Atkinson, Hannah Smith (Mrs. James), 7, 24, 32, 34, 41 n, 143

Atkinson, James, 2, 24, 36, 41 n, 54, 85, 102, 143

Backenstos, Lt. Col. Jacob B. (Backinsloch), 144, 152 n

Bailing & McKee, 148

Baker's Bay, 121 n

Baltimore, 35

Barclay, Dr. Forbes, 147, 153 n, 157

Barnhart, William H., 136, 141, 146, 147, 151 n, 155, 163

Beard, Capt. Edward (Ned), 112, 121 n, 130, 134, 146, 149, 156, 157, 163

Beaver Creek, 63

Bell, J. Stanislaw, 6

Bennett, Bob, 162

Bently, S., 145, 152 n

Bessell, Lieut. USN (Bissell), 145, 152 n

Birds store, 72

Black republicans, 165, 166 n

Blackhawk, 145, 152 n

Bond, James, 38, 40, 43 n, 46 n, 119 n, 236

Booker & Brand, 74, 75

Brickhead-Pearce, 38, 119 n

Brierly, Dr. 107, 111

Brinswade, 26

Brisbine, John, 147

Brown, Richard, 85

Bryant, William Cullen, 27, 43 n

Burns, Dan, 145, 148, 152 n, 163

Burns, Hugh, 2, 130, 133, 135, 136, 137, 138, 139, 141, 145, 151 n, 152 n, 153 n, 157, 160, 160 n, 161, 163, 166, 166 n

Bush, Asahel, 252 n, 160 n

California
climate, 27, 35, 39, 40, 47, 56, 58, 61, 62, 65, 96
destination, 9, 12, 17, 19, 22, 173-186
government, 27
labor, 27, 37
lack of amenities, 28, 32, 92, 97
mails, 9, 34, 38, 40
scenery, 32, 97, 183

California, 21, 24, 42 n

Candles, 85, 86, 88, 90, 94, 97, 105, 116, 124
adamantine, 33, 34, 36, 43 n, 88
sperm, 33
tallow, 61

Canemah (Canimah), 145, 152 n

Cape Hatteras, 173

Cape May, 110

Cape St. Lucas, 22, 184

Carson Valley, 98

Cass, Lewis, 7, 41 n

Catherine, 85, 86, 88, 94, 105

Cauly, Dr., 79, 80, 81

Chagres, 1, 9, 13, 21, 22, 23, 29, 41 n, 52, 95, 139, 173, 174, 175

Charleston, 8, 9, 174

Chester, 13

China, 93, 100, 141, 146, 153 n

Clark, Angel & Hoyt (Abernethy, Clarke), 145, 152 n

Clatsop Beach, 160 n

Cobb, Ned, 95

Cochran, G. (Cockran or Corkan), 66, 67, 69, 70, 71, 79

Codman, Capt., 13, 23

Collens, Capt. Jerry, 156, 157, 163

Collins, Tom, 145, 156, 157, 163

Coloma, 63, 119 n

Colum, James, 152 n

Columbia, 152 n

Columbia River, 113, 114, 116, 121 n, 125, 128, 152 n, 156, 157, 160 n, 165

Corbett, Henry W., 151 n

Corwin, Col. James, 5

Corwin, Thomas, 5, 124, 127, 142

Corwin, William, 6, 124, 142

Couch, Capt. John H., 163, 166 n

Creesy, Capt. Josiah P., 153 n

Crescent City, 15, 41 n

Cross, Joseph, 91, 98

Cross & Hobson, 1, 29, 30, 32, 34, 37, 40, 42 n, 51, 58, 74, 75, 81, 86, 88, 90, 92, 94, 97, 98, 107, 108, 114, 119 n, 124, 135

Cruces, 13, 19, 41 n, 175, 178, 179, 180

Curlett, John, 13, 33, 34, 43 n, 54, 61, 87, 88, 91, 151 n

Curlett, Mrs. John, 87, 89, 91, 93

Daguerreotypes, 123, 128, 131, 151 n, 155

Dalles, The, 153 n, 160 n, 162, 164

Deady, Matthew, 160 n

Deer Creek, 88

Dover's powders, 80, 119 n

Drugs, 33, 43 n, 113, 117, 118, 131, 149, 150

Dryer, Thomas G., 145, 152 n

Dungan, A. S. (Abe), 35, 114, 117, 120 n, 123, 128, 135, 149, 162

E. A. Spafford, 112, 114, 116, 118, 121 n

Eldorado, excerpts, 173-186

Elephant, see the, 21, 42 n, 98, 162

Ellicott, Grandmother, *see* Mrs. Nathan Tyson

Ellicott Mills, 62, 119 n, 120 n

Ellis, Chas., 38

Emigration, 97, 100, 104, 109, 117, 147, 158, 165, 180, 185

Emory, William Hemsley, 27, 43 n

Evans, George, 85, 120 n
Falcon, 8, 9, 10, 15, 19, 41 n, 52, 54,
  173-175, 179
Feather River, 119 n
Fendall, 132
Fenwick, A. F., 145
Ferdinand, 35
Ferris, Ned, 86
Fisher, George, 91
Flanders, Capt. George H., 163 n,
  166 n
Fleas, 55, 148
Flying Cloud, 149, 153 n
Foley, Jim, 62, 63
Folsom, Lake, 119 n
Fords Bar, 82
Fort Vancouver, 2, 116, 139, 140
Frémont, John Charles, 27, 43 n, 55,
  58, 120 n
Gaines, Gov. John P., 126, 145, 151 n,
  166 n
Gambling, 28, 43 n, 45, 72, 92, 99, 102
General Warren, 158, 160 n
George, Bill, 86
George, Robert, 123, 141, 151 n
George & Martha, 121 n, 156, 157
Georgetown, 2, 56, 62, 63, 78, 79, 80,
  81, 83, 119 n
Gibson, George, 123, 134, 151 n
Gold
  claims, 54, 65, 72, 77, 83, 109, *see
    also* Oregon Canyon, Otter
    Creek
  digs, 51, 54, 58, 62, 64, 65, 71, 76, 90,
    98, *see also* Mormon Island
  discovery in California, 42 n, 52,
    56, 63, 88, 119 n
  discovery in Nevada, 111
  discovery in Oregon, 124, 125, 129,
    130, 132, 145, 147, 151 n
  life at the mines, 62, 63, 76-78,
    79-81, 83
  machinery, 25, 26, 30, 46, 64, 78
  placer mining, 27, 39, 60, 64

  samples, 32, 60, 61, 78, 81, 108, 111,
    175
  worth, 31, 67, 68, 69, 144
Gold Hunter, 118
Gorgona, 19, 21, 27, 177, 178, 179, 180
Greeley, Horace, 23, 42 n
Greenmount Cemetery, 143
Grey Eagle, 21
Gwin, William M., 95, 120 n
Halowell, "young," 7, 41 n
Hambleton, Jessie, 107
Hamilton, Tom, 162
Handy, Bill, 85
Harriet, 156
Harrises, 145
Harry Carson & Cox, 54
Havana, 9, 11, 12, 174
Hayden and Cole, 90
Hays, Maj., 13, 41 n
Hedrick, Mr., 26
Henderson, Mr., 114
Hensley—Bankers, 88
High, William, 54, 67, 68, 69, 71, 79,
  80, 83, 119 n
Hobson, George, 85, 86, 95
Hobson, Capt. James, 33, 42 n, 106,
  107, 110, 138
Hobson, Mrs. Capt. James, 135, 151 n
Hobson, Joseph, 1, 26, 27, 29, 31, 32,
  33, 42 n, 46, 72, 76, 89, 106, 107,
  109, 110, 111, 135
Hobson, William, 1, 13, 26, 33, 39, 40,
  42 n, 47, 85, 95
Hogan, Gilbert, 72, 79
Hoit, Capt., 134
Hooper, John, 112
Hopkins, 141
Hopper, Mr., 101
Hudsons Bay Co., 2, 114, 121 n, 153 n,
  159, 160 n, 165
Humboldt Bar, 160 n
Hussey, Bond & Hale, 139
Illness
  ague, 13, 41 n, 108

"bile," 41 n
Chagres fever, 41 n, 86
cholera, 12, 41 n, 114, 118, 174, 181
dysentery, 31, 99, 102, 112, 141
"fever of the country," 34, 78, 87,
   89, 93, 96, 99, 100, 101, 106, 126
insect bites, 89, 91, 93, 96
poison oak, 98, 102, 120 n
Indians
   artifacts, 155-156, 166 n
   beads, 155-156, 157, 166 n
   California, 40, 61, 64, 69, 102, 111
   Oregon, 113, 116, 117, 145, 160 n, 166 n
Ice, 99, 105, 120 n
Iddings, Ned, 72, 73, 77, 81, 83, 100,
   108, 111
Iona, 106, 110
Ives, David, 95
Jakes, Mr., 54
James Conner, 161
Janny, Jonathan, 14
Jericho, 17, 23, 32, 34, 42 n
John C. Demerest, 156, 157
Juliet, 157, 160 n
Keman, Jimmy, 35
Kemps, Charly, 88
King, A. N., 160 n
King, Thomas Butler, 28, 32, 43 n,
   123, 126, 127, 129, 131
King, William M., 144, 151 n
King & Cross, 134
Klamath Mines, 129, 130, 151 n
Lady Adams, 35
Landstreet, 95
Lane, Gen. Joseph, 163, 166 n
Lane, Richard, 159, 160 n
Laura Bevan, 85, 86, 88, 105, 110, 111
Lea, James, 30, 32, 34, 35, 40, 43 n,
   48, 97, 100, 101, 105, 108, 110, 111,
   169
Lee, Barton, 104
Lee, Betsy, 95
Lindsay, Mr. I., 33
Linn City, *see* Lynn City

Lizzie, *see* Smith, Elizabeth Brooke
   Tyson
Locofocos, 33, 43 n, 152 n
Lot Whitcomb, 145, 152 n
Louisiana, 123, 129
Lovejoy, Asa, 160 n
Lowenstein & Gibson & Co., 134,
   136, 151 n
Lynn City (West Linn), 144, 152 n,
   153 n, 163, 165
Lynch law (Judge Linch), 100, 120 n
Madonna, 166 n
Mail
   by acquaintances, 30, 31, 33, 36, 38,
      56, 59, 74, 82, 131
   in California, 30, 34, 37, 40
   ineffective postal system, 38,
      52-53
   sending of gold by JMS, 52, 60, 78,
      81, 108
   via *Falcon*, 8, 11, 14
   via Isthmus of Panama, 52-53
Main, Mr., 135
Marge, 163
Marsh, Thomas, 13, 25, 42 n, 56, 61
Marshal, 156
Marshall, John, 119 n
Marshalship, 2, 124, 126, 127, 129, 132
Martin, George, 7
Maryland, 166 n
Massy, Dr., 131
Mastier, William, 10
Matthews, James, 32
May and Goldsmith, 144
May, Lewis, 144, 147, 152 n
Maxwell, Dr., 156
Mazatlan, 21, 22, 24, 42 n, 182, 183
McDuffie, Mr., 29
McKim, 35
McKinley, A., 153 n
McLoughlin, Dr. John, 2, 21, 114, 156,
   164-165, 166 n
McMullen, Dr. (Dr. McMillan), 17,
   19, 22

McNulty & Stambough, 26
Merchandising/trading
  auction, 48, 90, 123n
  bolt, 39
  business conditions, 39, 90, 100,
    101, 102, 104, 105, 109, 124, 136,
    137-138, 146, 156
  by lots, 46
  on board, 90
  prices, 33, 34, 36, 39, 47, 91, 105
  rent, 34, 47, 54, 100
  sell blind, 90
Merchantman, 121n, 146
Merrill, R., 88
Milton, 144, 152n
Milwaukie, 152n
Mississippi River, 12
Missouri Hotel, 40, 43n, 105
Monterey, 1, 25, 26, 27, 29, 32
Monumental City, 162
Moore, Charles, 89, 125, 126, 151n
Moore, Robert, 152n, 158, 160n, 165
Mormon Island, 2, 25, 27, 30, 31, 32,
    42n, 60, 62, 119n
Moro Castle, 11, 174
Mosquitoes, 14, 96
Multnomah City, 136, 146, 151n, 153n,
    155, 158, 160n, 164, 166n
Murrys, 145
Negroes, 29, 37
New Helvetia, 102
New Orleans, 9, 10, 11, 12, 14, 15-17, 19,
    36, 41n, 174
New York Tribune, 12, 23, 41n, 81
Nicaragua road, 95
Nine Mile House, 62, 119n
Norris & Co., 135, 138
Norris, Shubrick, 144, 151n, 163
Norris, William, 85
North Fork and Yuba Hotel, 1, 37, 39,
    47, 89
Norton, Zachariah D., 144, 147, 152n,
    158
Ober and McConky, 128

Oil speculation, 95
Ogden, 163
Oregon, 2, 100, 112, 114, 118, 123, 124,
    125, 127, 129, 130, 131, 132, 148, 152,
    156-159, 162-163
  business, 2, 114, 116, 117, 118, 119, 124,
    125, 134, 138, 141, 158
  gold mines, 124, 125, 127, 129, 130,
    132, 133, 138, 142, 145, 147, 151n,
    152n
  government, 144, 158, 160n, 163,
    166n
Oregon, 17, 24, 42n, 134
Oregon Canyon, 58, 64, 65
Oregon City, 2, 52, 114, 116, 117, 118,
    132, 133, 147, 151n, 152n, 153n, 157,
    159, 160n, 163
Oregon Steam Navigation Co., 151n
Oregonian, 152n
Orus (Oris), 13, 18, 41n
Osceola, 13, 41n, 56
Otter Creek, 59, 60, 65, 69, 72, 75, 77,
    80, 82, 83, 108
Pacific City, 113, 116, 121n
Pacific Mail Steamship Line, *see
    also Falcon*, 52
Panama, 17, 19, 21, 23, 24, 135, 186
Panama City, 13, 15, 18, 19, 22, 24, 46,
    91, 103, 104, 108, 162, 175, 178, 179,
    180, 181, 183
Panama, Isthmus of, 1, 13, 18, 19-21,
    37, 52, 142, 175-180
Pearce (Pierce), Ned, 72, 73, 77, 80,
    83, 93, 100, 108, 111, 119n
Placer Times, 33, 49-51, 52, 160n
Polallio, 145, 152n
Polk, President James K., 27, 166n
Porter, 54
Portland, 114, 117, 118, 133, 136, 141, 144,
    147, 152n, 158, 163, 166n
Portland Steam Packet Co., 160n
Priest, Mr., 26
Quicksilver, 21, 32, 42n
Radle, Dr., 25

Republic, 138
Rio Grande, 179, 182
Robinson, Wm., 107, 111
Rose-Merrill & Dodge (or Lodge), 88
Sacramento
  "The Amphibious," 51, 72, 77
  business, 2, 28, 32, 34, 36, 39-40, 47-48, 88, 90, 99, 100, 105, 107, 109, 112, 116
  floods, 2, 39, 47-51, 77, 98, 120 n
  growth, 28, 33-34, 36, 90, 102
  location, description, 1, 2, 26, 28, 33, 37, 39, 47, 77, 98, 102-103, 105, 126
  population, 28, 39, 103
  provisions, 34, 39, 48, 91, 98
  shipping, 28, 34, 39
Sacramento River, 28, 35, 49-51, 152 n, 106
Saint Charles Hotel, 10, 12, 36, 41 n
Salem, 165
San Blas, 21, 24, 182
San Diego, 184-185
San Francisco, 1, 13, 15, 19, 27-28, 32, 54, 62, 107, 108, 138, 146-148, 157, 159, 185-186
  destination, 18, 19, 21, 45, 104
  lack of amenities, 28, 32, 40
San Jose (San Hosa), 29, 32, 43 n, 127, 131, 183
Sanders & Dungan, 161
Sanders, Beverley (Saunders), 107, 111, 120 n, 131, 142
Sandwich Island, 98, 136
Sandy Hook, 8
Savannah, 9
Scott, 54, 62, 72, 119 n
Sea Gull, 134, 157, 160 n
Senator, 35
Sequin, 152 n
Shoal Water Bay, 113, 114, 116, 121 n
Shore, John, 86
Sierra Nevadas, 35, 47, 97, 98, 185

Silas Baldwin, 85
Silas Richards, 137
Simpson, 163
Sims, John A., 146, 153 n, 164
Siwashes, 145, 152 n
Skenk, Capt., 9
Skinner, Judge Alonzo A., 163, 166 n
Skukum Chuck, 145, 152 n
Slavery, 29, 43 n, 120 n, 166 n
Smith, Anthony Marsh (Tony), 32, 37, 40, 43 n, 51, 58, 84, 86, 87, 88, 93, 96, 97, 105, 107, 110, 111, 170
Smith, Catherine Ellen, 95, 97, 120 n, 170
Smith, Catherine Marsh (Mrs. Matthew Smith), 10, 14, 21, 25, 29, 35, 37, 41 n, 43 n, 48, 54, 55, 60, 89, 93, 98, 105, 107, 110, 118, 125, 170
Smith, Elizabeth Brooke Tyson (Mrs. J. Marsh Smith), 1, 2, 8, 9, 11, 14, 15, 18, 22-23, 24, 25, 31, 34, 35, 36, 39-40, 46, 48, 51, 54, 56, 58, 59, 61, 76, 79, 81, 82, 84, 87, 89, 92, 93, 95, 96, 97, 99, 103, 105, 106, 107, 110, 112, 113, 114, 116, 117, 123-124, 126, 128, 130, 131, 132, 135, 140, 143, 158, 170, 171
Smith, Gilbert T. (Gilly), 7, 31, 34, 36, 38, 41 n, 48, 51, 55, 56, 60, 82, 84, 85, 89, 93, 97, 99, 110, 114, 123, 125, 126, 128, 133, 143, 171
Smith, Hannah Ann, *see* Atkinson, Hannah Smith
Smith, John, 9, 12
Smith, John Marsh
  en route to the Isthmus, 5-15
  from Panama to California, 19-24
  in San Francisco, 27-33
  in Sacramento, 33-48
  at the mines, 56-84
  en route to Oregon, 112-118
  in Oregon, 118-141
  return to Baltimore, 142

Smith, Maj., 9, 10

Smith, Martha Tyson, 159, 160 n, 171

Smith, Mary Marsh, 95, 120 n, 170

Smith, Matthew, 37, 42 n, 43 n, 48, 55, 60, 85, 106, 110, 170

Smith, Sarah R. (Sally), 95, 97, 99, 120 n, 170

Smith, Thomas M. (Tommy), 31, 34, 36, 43 n, 48, 51, 55, 56, 60, 82, 89, 93, 97, 99, 114, 123, 126, 128, 133, 143, 171

Smith, Thomas Marsh (Thomas M.), 13, 25, 34, 38, 40, 41 n, 42 n, 58, 61, 84, 85, 86, 88, 89, 93, 94-95, 98, 111, 124, 127, 135, 142, 170

Smith & Atkinson, 43 n, 84, 151

Smith & Curlett, 36, 43 n, 116

Smith & Suydam, 90, 101

Soap, 33, 91, 139

Souvies Island (Sauvie Island), 146, 152 n

Spectator, 152 n

Squatters Riots, 106-107, 109, 111, 120 n

Stabler, 111

Stark, Sam, 108

Starr, Minstrom & Co., 140

Statesman, 145, 152 n

Steel, Samuel, 86

Steinberger, 29

Stevens, Nathan, J., 119 n

Stillinger, 35

Strobel, Pater, 162

Success, 145, 156

Sugar, 134, 136, 139, 145, 146, 159

Summer Hill, 95

Surrey, 149

Sutter, John A., 119 n

Sutter's Fort (Fort Sutters), 48, 49, 119 n

Sutter's Mill, 2, 42 n, 62

Suydam, James, 2, 90, 92, 101, 102, 120 n

Suydam, Lambert, 90, 92, 101, 120 n

Swain, George, 52

Taboga, 180

Talbott, William A., 13, 14, 27, 33, 42 n, 55, 61, 89, 95, 99, 101

Tarquina, 114

Taylor, Bayard, 12, 23, 41 n, 173

Taylor, President Zachary, 41 n, 43 n, 107, 120 n, 151 n

Thompson, R. R., 144, 145, 151 n, 163

Todd & Co., 134

Todhunter, Joseph, 37, 40, 43 n, 59

Tompkins, 158

TransIsthmus Railroad, 120 n, 180

Tucker, Cooper and Co., 120 n

Tumwata, 144, 151 n

Tumwater, 145, 152 n

Tyson, Anne, 7, 25, 41 n, 93, 95, 99, 107, 108, 111, 127, 131, 170

Tyson, Elisha, 119 n

Tyson, Frederick, 1, 2, 7, 8, 12, 15, 17-18, 19, 21, 22-24, 27, 30, 31-32, 36, 39, 40, 41 n, 46-47, 54, 58, 59, 60, 62, 72, 73, 76, 77, 78, 79-81, 83, 84, 86, 87, 88, 89, 90, 93, 95, 96, 97, 101, 103, 106, 107, 109, 123, 143, 170

Tyson, Harriet (Mrs. James), 18, 42 n, 54, 58, 75, 79, 81, 93, 95, 97, 106, 143, 170

Tyson, Henry, 7, 33, 41 n, 170

Tyson, Isabelle (Belle), 93, 107, 108, 110, 111, 120 n, 127, 131, 170

Tyson, James, 13, 18, 24, 34, 36, 42 n, 54, 61, 75, 78, 97, 143, 170

Tyson, Lucy, 93, 120 n, 170

Tyson, Nathan, 13, 25, 40, 42 n, 46, 51, 56, 58, 73, 84, 85, 87, 88, 89, 90, 93, 103, 107, 109, 113, 118, 120 n, 127, 142, 143, 170

Tyson, Mrs. Nathan (Martha Ellicott), 13, 48, 119 n, 121 n, 166 n, 170

Tyson, Robert, 13, 33, 38, 39, 42 n, 58, 61, 86, 88, 93, 95, 112, 117, 118, 124, 131, 143, 170

Tyson & Dungan, 33, 42 n, 110, 116, 143

Umpqua River, 145

Unicorn, 17, 22

Union Insurance Co. of N.Y., 92, 101, 120 n

Van Tempsky, Capt. Gustav, 6

Vernon, 73-75, 119 n

Walnut Hill, 105, 107, 110

Warfield, Henry (Harry), 15, 28, 42 n

Webb, William H., 120 n

Webb-Quiller, George W., 146

Webster, Daniel, 127, 151 n

Wells, Fargo & Co., 151 n

Wethered, Jas., 39, 43 n, 47

Wethered, John, 85, 93, 98, 102, 120 n

White Sulphur Springs, 95, 120 n

Willamette River, 2, 117, 118, 121 n, 125, 130, 145, 147, 151 n, 152 n, 153 n, 160 n, 165

Willapa Bay, 121 n

Williams, 56, 59

Williams, Thomas, 37, 43 n, 62, 70

Williams, William (Bill), 54, 59, 62, 70

Wilson, Gen. Jno., 6

Wine, 21, 80

Winter & Latimer, 39, 147, 153 n

Winton & Colman, 158

Wright, Dr., 62, 66, 79

Yaquina Bay, 160 n

Yuba River, 51, 55

Dear Lizzie is designed by Susan Applegate, with maps drawn by John Tomlinson. The composition is by Irish Setter, and the printing is by Thomson-Shore. The typeface is Walbaum, originally cut by J. E. Walbaum in the first years of the 19th century; it is a German varient of a "modern" face, representing the ultimate adaptation of the roman alphabet to the rectangular environment of lead type. The paper is Warren's Olde Style, which is acid free.